LIQUID LOVE

On the Frailty of Human Bonds

ZYGMUNT BAUMAN

polity

First published in 2003 by Polity Press in association with Blackwell Publishing Ltd

Reprinted 2003, 2004 (twice), 2005, 2008 (twice)

Polity Press
65 Bridge Street
Cambridge CB2 1UR, UK

Polity Press
350 Main Street
Malden, MA 02148, USA

A catalogue record for this book is available from the British Library.

Library of Congress Cataloging-in-Publication Data

Bauman, Zygmunt.
Liquid love : on the frailty of human bonds / Zygmunt Bauman.
    p. cm.
Includes index.
ISBN 978-0-7456-2488-4—ISBN 978-0-7456-2489-1 (pbk.)
1. Social isolation. 2. Social distance. 3. Interpersonal relations.
4. Intergroup relations. I. Title.
HM1131 .B38 2003
302.5'45—dc21

                                    2002014474

Typeset in 11 on 13 pt Sabon
by Kolam Information Services Pvt. Ltd, Pondicherry, India
Printed and bound in United States by Odyssey Press Inc., Gonic, New Hampshire

For further information on Polity, visit our website: www.polity.co.uk

Contents

v

Foreword

Ulrich, the hero of Robert Musil's great novel, was – as the title of the novel announced – *Der Mann ohne Eigenschaften*: the man without qualities. Having no qualities of his own, whether inherited or acquired once and for all and undetachable, Ulrich had to compose whatever quality he might have wished to have by his own effort, using his own wits and acumen; but none of these qualities were guaranteed to last indefinitely in a world full of confusing signals, prone to change fast and in a way no one expected.

The hero of this book is Der Mann ohne Verwandtschaften – the man with no bonds, and particularly no bonds as fixed as the kinship bonds used to be in Ulrich's time. Having no bonds that are unbreakable and attached once and for all, the hero of this book – the denizen of our liquid modern society – and his successors today must tie together whatever bonds they want to use as a link to engage with the rest of the human world by their own efforts with the help of their own skills and dedication. Unbound, they must connect... None of the connections that come to fill the gap left by the absent or mouldy bonds are, however, guaranteed to last. Anyway, they need to be only loosely tied, so that they can be untied again, with little delay, when the settings change – as in liquid modernity they surely will, over and over again.

The uncanny frailty of human bonds, the feeling of insecurity that frailty inspires, and the conflicting desires that feeling prompts to tighten the bonds yet keep them loose is what this book tries to unravel, record and grasp.

Lacking Musil's sharpness of vision, richness of palette and subtlety of brushstrokes – in fact any of his exquisite talents that made *Der Mann ohne Eigenschaften* into the definitive portrait of the modern man – I have to confine myself to drafting a portfolio of rough and fragmentary sketches, rather than try a full, let alone the definitive likeness. The most I can hope for is an identity kit, a composite picture that may contain as many gaps and blank spots as filled-up sections. Even that final composition, though, will be an unfinished task, left to the readers to complete.

The principal hero of this book is human *relationship*. This book's central characters are men and women, our contemporaries, despairing at being abandoned to their own wits and feeling easily disposable, yearning for the security of togetherness and for a helping hand to count on in a moment of trouble, and so desperate to 'relate'; yet wary of the state of 'being related' and particularly of being related 'for good', not to mention forever – since they fear that such a state may bring burdens and cause strains they neither feel able nor are willing to bear, and so may severely limit the freedom they need – yes, your guess is right – to relate...

In our world of rampant 'individualization' relationships are mixed blessings. They vacillate between sweet dream and a nightmare, and there is no telling when one turns into the other. Most of the time the two avatars cohabit – though at different levels of consciousness. In a liquid modern setting of life, relationships are perhaps the most common, acute, deeply felt and troublesome incarnations of ambivalence. This is, we may argue, why they are firmly placed at the very heart of the attention of liquid modern individuals-by-decree and perched at the top of their life agenda.

'Relationship' is these days the hottest talk of the town and ostensibly the sole game in town worth playing, despite its notorious risks. Some sociologists, used to composing theories out of questionnaire statistics and the commonsensical beliefs such stat-

istics record, hurry to conclude tha
out for friendships, bonds, togethern
ever (as if following Martin Heide
themselves to consciousness only through the frustration they
cause – going bust, disappearing, behaving out of character or
otherwise belying their nature), human attention tends nowadays
to be focused on the satisfactions that relationships are hoped to
bring precisely because somehow they have not been found fully
and truly satisfactory; and if they do satisfy, the price of the
satisfaction they bring has often been found to be excessive and
unacceptable. In their famous experiment, Miller and Dollard saw
their laboratory rats ascending the peak of excitement and agitation when 'the adiance equalled the abiance' – that is, when the
threat of electric shock and the promise of tasty food were finely
balanced...

No wonder that 'relationships' are one of the main engines of
the present-day 'counselling boom'. The complexity is too dense,
too stubborn and too difficult to unpack or unravel for individuals
to do the job unassisted. The agitation of Miller and Dollard's rats
all too often collapsed into a paralysis of action. An inability to
choose between attraction and repulsion, between hopes and fears,
rebounded as an incapacity to act. Unlike the rats, humans who
find themselves in such circumstances may turn for help to the
expert counsellors offering their services, for a fee. What they hope
to hear from the counsellors is how to square the circle: to eat the
cake and have it, to cream off the sweet delights of relationship
while omitting its bitter and tougher bits; how to force relationship
to empower without disempowering, enable without disabling,
fulfilling without burdening...

The experts are willing to oblige, confident that the demand for
their counsels will never run dry since no amount of counselling
could ever make a circle non-circular and thus amenable to being
squared... Their counsels abound, though more often than not
they do little more than raise common practice to the level of
common knowledge, and that in turn to the heights of learned,
authoritative theory. Grateful recipients of advice browse through
'relationship' columns of glossy monthlies and weeklies and

weekly supplements of serious and less serious dailies to hear what they have been wishing to hear from people 'in the know', since they were too timid or ashamed to aver it in their own name; to pry into the doings and goings on of 'others like them' and draw whatever comfort they can manage to draw from the knowledge endorsed-by-experts that they are not alone in their lonely efforts to cope with the quandary.

And so the readers learn, from other readers' experience recycled by the counsellors, that they may try 'top pocket relationships', of the sort they 'can bring out when they need them' but push deep down in the pocket when they do not. Or that relationships are like Ribena: imbibed in concentration, they are nauseating and may prove dangerous to their health – like Ribena, relations should be diluted when consumed. Or that SDCs – 'semi-detached couples' – are to be praised as 'relationship revolutionaries who have burst the suffocating couple bubble'. Or that relationships, like cars, should undergo regular MOTs to make sure that they are still roadworthy. All in all, what they learn is that commitment, and particularly long-term commitment, is the trap that the endeavour 'to relate' should avoid more than any other danger. One expert counsellor informs readers that 'when committing yourself, however half-heartedly, remember that you are likely to be closing the door to other romantic possibilities which may be more satisfying and fulfilling.' Another expert sounds blunter yet: 'Promises of commitment are meaningless in the long term ... Like other investments, they wax and wane.' And so, if you wish 'to relate', keep your distance; if you want fulfilment from your togetherness, do not make or demand commitments. Keep all doors open at any time.

The residents of Leonia, one of Italo Calvino's *Invisible Cities*, would say, if asked, that their passion is 'the enjoyment of new and different things'. Indeed – each morning they 'wear brand-new clothing, take from the latest model refrigerator still unopened tins, listening to the last-minute jingles from the most up-to-date radio'. But each morning 'the remains of yesterday's Leonia await the garbage truck' and one is right to wonder whether the Leonians' true passion is not instead 'the joy of expelling, discarding, cleansing themselves of a recurrent impurity'. Otherwise why would street cleaners be 'welcomed like angels', even if their mission is 'surrounded by respectful silence', and understandably so – 'once things have been cast off nobody wants to have to think about them further.'

Let us think . . .

Are not the residents of our liquid modern world, just like the residents of Leonia, worrying about one thing while speaking of another? They say that their wish, passion, aim or dream is 'to relate'. But are they not in fact mostly concerned with how to prevent their relations from curdling and clotting? Are they indeed after relationships that hold, as they say they are, or do they, more than anything else, desire those relationships to be light and loose, so that after the pattern of Richard Baxter's riches that were supposed to 'lie on the shoulders like a light cloak' they could 'be thrown aside at any moment'? When everything is said and done, what sort of advice do they truly want: how to tie the relationship, or how – just in case – to take it apart without harm and with a clear conscience? There is no easy answer to that question, though the question needs to be asked and will go on being asked, as the denizens of the liquid modern world go on smarting under the crushing burden of the most ambivalent of the many ambivalent tasks they daily confront.

Perhaps the very idea of 'relationship' adds to the confusion. However hard the hapless relation-seekers and their counsellors try, the notion resists being fully and truly cleansed of its disturbing and worrying connotations. It stays pregnant with vague threats and sombre premonitions; it tells of the pleasures of to-getherness in one breath with the horrors of enclosure. Perhaps this is why, rather than report their experience and prospects in terms of 'relating' and 'relationships', people speak ever more often (aided and abetted by the learned advisers) of connections, of 'connecting' and 'being connected'. Instead of talking about partners, they prefer to speak of 'networks'. What are the merits of the language of 'connectedness' that are missed by the language of 'relationships'?

Unlike 'relations', 'kinships', 'partnerships' and similar notions that make salient the mutual engagement while excluding or passing over in silence its opposite, the disengagement, 'network' stands for a matrix for simultaneously connecting and disconnecting; networks are unimaginable without both activities being simultaneously enabled. In a network, connecting and disconnecting are equally legitimate choices, enjoy the same status and carry the same importance. No point in asking which of the two complementary activities constitutes 'the essence' of network! 'Network' suggests moments of 'being in touch' interspersed with periods of free roaming. In a network, connections are entered on demand, and can be broken at will. An 'undesirable, yet unbreakable' relationship is the very possibility that makes 'relating' as treacherous as it feels. An 'undesirable connection', however, is an oxymoron: connections may be, and are, broken well before they start being detested.

Connections are 'virtual relations'. Unlike old-fashioned relationships (not to mention 'committed' relationships, let alone long-term commitments), they seem to be made to the measure of a liquid modern life setting where 'romantic possibilities' (and not only 'romantic' ones) are supposed and hoped to come and go with ever greater speed and in never thinning crowds, stampeding each other off the stage and out-shouting each other with promises 'to be more satisfying and fulfilling'. Unlike 'real relationships', 'virtual relationships' are easy to enter and to exit. They look smart and clean, feel easy to use and user-friendly, when compared with the heavy, slow-moving, inert messy 'real stuff'. A twenty-eight-year-old man from Bath, interviewed in connection with the rapidly growing popularity of computer dating at the expense of singles bars and lonely-heart columns, pointed to one decisive advantage of electronic relation: 'you can always press "delete"'.

As if obedient to Gresham's law, virtual relations (renamed 'connections') set the pattern which drives out all other relationships. That does not make the men and women who surrender to the pressure happy; hardly happier than the practising of pre-virtual relations made them. You gain something, you lose something else.

As Ralph Waldo Emerson pointed out, when skating on thin ice your salvation is in speed. When the quality lets you down, you tend to seek redemption in quantity. If 'commitments are mean-ingless' while relations cease to be trustworthy and are unlikely to last, you are inclined to swap partnerships for networks. Once you have done it, however, settling down turns out even more difficult (and so more off-putting) than before – you now miss the skills that would or could make it work. Being on the move, once a privilege and an achievement, becomes a must. Keeping up speed, once an exhilarating adventure, turns into an exhausting chore. Most importantly, that nasty uncertainty and that vexing confu-sion, supposed to be chased away thanks to speed, refuse to go. The facility of disengagement and termination-on-demand do not reduce the risks; they only distribute them, together with the anxieties they exhale, differently.

This book is dedicated to the risks and anxieties of living to-gether, and apart, in our liquid modern world.

Falling In and Out of Love

'My dear friend, I send you a small work of which one could say, not unjustly, that it has neither head nor tail, since everything in it is on the contrary a head and a tail, alternatively and reciprocally. Consider, I beg you, the admirable convenience such a combination offers to all – to you, to me, and the reader. We may cut short – I my musings, you the text, the reader his reading; because I do not hold the tiring will of any of them endlessly to a superfluous plot. Take out one disc, and two pieces of that tortuous fantasy will fall back together without difficulty. Chop out many fragments, and you'll find that each one can exist on its own. Hoping that some of its stretches will please and amuse you, I dare to dedicate to you the whole snake.'

This is how Charles Baudelaire introduced *Le spleen de Paris* to his readers. What a pity that he did. Had he not, I myself would have wished to compose the same or a similar preamble to what is about to follow. But he did – and I can *only* quote. Walter Benjamin, of course, would strike out the word 'only' from the last sentence. And so would I, on second thoughts.

'Chop out many fragments, and you'll find that each one can exist on its own.' The fragments flowing from under Baudelaire's pen did; whether the scattered thought-snippets collected below will – is not mine, but the reader's right to decide.

1

In the family of thoughts, there are dwarfs aplenty. This is why logic and method were invented, and once discovered were gratefully embraced by the thinkers of thoughts. Midgets may hide, and in the end forget their puniness amid the mighty splendour of marching columns and battle arrays. Once ranks are closed, who will notice how tiny the soldiers are? You can make an awesomely powerful-looking army by lining up in fighting order rows upon rows of pygmies...

Perhaps, if only to please the methodology addicts, I should have done the same with these chopped-out fragments. But since I do not have enough time left for the finishing of such a task, it would be foolish of me to think of the rank order first and leave the call-up for later...

On second thoughts: perhaps the time at my disposal seems too short not because of my old age, but because the older you are the better you know that however big the thoughts may seem, they will never be big enough to embrace, let alone keep hold of, the bountiful prodigality of human experience. What we know, wish to know, struggle to know, must try to know about love or rejection, being alone or together and dying together or alone – can all that be streamlined, put in order, match the standards of consistency, cohesiveness and completeness set for the lesser matters? Perhaps it can – in the infinity of time, that is.

Is it not so that when everything is said about the matters most important to human life, the most important things remain unsaid?

Love and death, the two principal characters of this story, with neither a plot nor a denouement but condensing most of life's sound and fury, admit this kind of musing/writing/reading more than any other.

Ivan Klima says: there is little that comes so close to death as fulfilled love. Each appearance of either of the two is a one-off, but also once-and-for-all appearance, brooking no repetition, allowing no appeal and promising no reprieve. Each one must, and does, stand 'on its own'. Each one is born for the first time, or born again, whenever it enters, always sprouting from nowhere, from the darkness of non-being without past or future. Each one, each time, begins from the beginning, laying bare the superfluity of past plots and the vanity of all future plotting.

Neither love nor death can be entered twice; even less so than Heraclitus' river. They are, indeed, their own head and tails, being dismissive and negligent of all others.

Bronisław Malinowski used to sneer at the diffusionists for mistaking museum collections for genealogies; having seen cruder flint implements put in glass cases before the more refined ones, they spoke of 'tools' history'. That was, Malinowski jeered, as if one stone axe begat another in the same way as, say, *hipparion* gave birth, in the fullness of time, to *equus caballus*. The origins of horses can be traced to other horses, but tools are not ancestors or descendants of other tools. Tools, unlike horses, have no history of their own. They, one may say, punctuate human individual biographies and collective histories; they are effusions or sediments of such biographies and histories.

Much the same can be said of love and death. Kinship, affinity, causal links are all features of human selfhood and/or togetherness. Love and death have no history of their own. They are events in human time – each one a separate event, *not* connected (let alone connected *causally*) to other 'similar' events, unless in human compositions retrospectively eager to spot – to invent – the connections and comprehend the incomprehensible.

And so you cannot learn to love; nor can you learn to die. And you cannot learn the elusive – the non-existent, though keenly desired – art of avoiding their grip and keeping out of their way. Love and death will strike, come their time; only you have no inkling when that time is. Whenever it comes, it will take you unawares. Into your daily preoccupations, love and death will rise *ab nihilo* – out of nothingness. We are all likely, of course, to lean over backwards to become wise after the fact; we will try to trace back the antecedents, deploy the foolproof principle of a *post hoc* surely being the *propter hoc*, try to map a 'making sense' lineage of the event, and more often than not we will succeed. We need such success for the spiritual comfort it brings: it resurrects, even if in a roundabout way, the faith in the regularity of the world and the predictability of events, indispensable for sanity. It also conjures up an illusion of wisdom gained, of learning, and above all a wisdom one can learn, as one learns to use J. S. Mill's canons of induction, drive cars, eat with chopsticks instead of forks, or make a favourable impression on interviewers.

In the case of death, learning is admittedly confined to other people's experience and so it is an illusion *in extremis*. Other people's experience cannot be truly learned as experience; in the end-product of learning the object, one can never separate the original *Erlebnis* from the creative contribution of the subject's imaginative powers. Experience of others can be known only as a processed, interpreted story of what the others lived through. Perhaps some real-life cats have, like Tom of *Tom & Jerry* cartoons, nine lives or more, and perhaps some converts can come to believe in being born again – but the fact remains that death like birth happens only once; there is no way one can learn to 'do it properly next time' from an event never to be experienced again.

Love seems to enjoy a different status from the other one-off events.

Indeed, one can fall in love more than once, and some people pride themselves, or complain, that falling in and out of love comes to them (and some others they came to know in the process) all too easily. Everyone has heard stories of such particularly 'love-prone' or 'love-vulnerable' persons.

There are solid enough grounds to see love, and particularly the state of 'being in love', as – almost by its nature – a recurrent condition, amenable to repetition, even inviting repeated attempts. When pressed, most of us would name a number of times when we felt we had fallen in love and were in love. One can guess (but it will be an informed guess) that in our times the ranks of people who tend to attach the name of love to more than one of their life experiences, who would not vouch that the love they are currently experiencing is the last, and who expect there are more such experiences yet to come, is growing fast. If the guess proves right, one should not be amazed. After all, the romantic definition

4

of love as 'till death us do part' is decidedly out of fashion – having passed its use-by date because of the radical overhaul of the kinship structures it used to serve and from which it drew its vigour and self-importance. But the demise of that notion means, inevitably, the easing of the tests an experience must pass to be assigned as 'love'. Rather than more people rising to the high standards of love on more occasions, the standards have been lowered; as a result the set of experiences referred to by the love word has expanded enormously. One-night stands are talked about under the code name of 'making love'.

This sudden abundance and apparent availability of 'love experiences' may (and does) feed the conviction that love (falling in love, soliciting love) is a skill to be learned, and that the mastery of the skill grows with the number of experiments and assiduity of exercise. One may even (and one all too often does) believe that love-making skills are bound to grow as the experience accumulates; that the next love will be an experience yet more exhilarating than the one currently enjoyed, though not as thrilling or exciting as the one after next.

This is, though, another illusion ... The kind of knowledge that rises in volume as the string of love episodes grows longer is that of 'love' as sharp, short and shocking episodes, shot through by the *a priori* awareness of brittleness and brevity. The kinds of skills that are acquired are those of 'finishing quickly and starting from the beginning', of which, according to Søren Kierkegaard, Mozart's Don Giovanni was the archetypal virtuoso. But guided as he was by the compulsion to try again, and obsessed with preventing each successive attempt in the present from standing in the way of further trying, Don Giovanni was also an archetypal 'love impotent'. Were love the purpose of Don Giovanni's indefatigable searching and experimenting, the compulsion to experiment would defy the purpose. It is tempting to say that the effect of the ostensible 'acquisition of skills' is bound to be, as in Don Giovanni's case, the *de-learning* of love; a 'trained incapacity' for loving.

An outcome like this – the vengeance of love, so to speak, on those who dare to challenge its nature – could have been expected. One can learn to perform an activity where there is a set of invariable rules corresponding to a stable, monotonously repetitive setting that favours learning, memorizing and a subsequent 'going through motions'. In an unstable environment, retention and habit acquisition – the trademarks of successful learning – are not just counterproductive, but may prove to be fatal in their consequences. What, over and over again, proves lethal to the rats in city sewers – those highly intelligent creatures able to learn fast how to sieve out the nutritious snips from among the poisonous baits – is the element of instability, of rule defiance, inserted into the network of underground troughs and chutes by the irregular, unlearnable, unpredictable, truly impenetrable 'alterity' of other – human – intelligent creatures: creatures notorious for their penchant for breaking with routine and playing havoc with the distinction between the regular and the contingent. If that distinction is not upheld, learning (in as far as it is understood as the acquisition of useful habits) is out of the question. Those who persist in binding their actions by precedents, like the generals known to fight their last victorious war all over again, undertake suicidal risks and invite no end of troubles.

It belongs to the nature of love that – as Lucan observed two millennia ago and Francis Bacon repeated many centuries later – it cannot but mean giving hostages to fate.

In Plato's *Symposium*, Diotima of Mantinea (that is, in English translation, 'prophetess Fearthelord of Prophetville') pointed out to Socrates, with the latter's wholehearted agreement, that 'love is not for the beautiful, as you think'; 'It is for begetting and birth in the beautiful.' To love is to desire 'to beget and procreate', and so the lover 'seeks and goes about to find the beautiful thing in which he can beget'. In other words, it is not in craving after ready-made, complete and finished things that love finds its meaning – but in the urge to participate in the becoming of such things. Love is akin to transcendence; it is but another name for creative drive and as such is fraught with risks, as all creation is never sure where it is going to end.

In every love, there are at least two beings, each of them the great unknown in the equations of the other. This is what makes love feel like a caprice of fate – that eerie and mysterious future, impossible to be told in advance, to be pre-empted or staved off, to be speeded up or arrested. To love means opening up to that fate, that most sublime of all human conditions, one in which fear blends with joy into an alloy that no longer allows its ingredients to separate. Opening up to that fate means, in the ultimate account, admission of freedom into being: that freedom which is embodied in the Other, the companion in love. As Erich Fromm put it: 'Satisfaction in individual love cannot be attained...without true humility, courage, faith and discipline'; only to add right away, with sadness, that in 'a culture in which these qualities are rare, the attainment of the capacity to love must remain a rare achievement'.[1]

And so it does – in a consumer culture like ours, which favours products ready for instant use, quick fixes, instantaneous satisfaction, results calling for no protracted effort, foolproof recipes, all-risk insurance and money-back guarantees. The promise to learn the art of loving is a (false, deceitful, yet keenly wished to be true) promise to make 'love experience' in the likeness of other commodities, that allure and seduce by brandishing all such features and promise to take the waiting out of wanting, sweat out of effort and effort out of results.

Without humility and courage, no love. Both are required, in huge and constantly replenished supplies, whenever one enters an unexplored and unmapped land, and when love happens between two or more human beings it ushers them into such a territory.

Eros, as Levinas insists,[2] differs from possession and from power; it is neither a battle nor a fusion – and not knowledge either.

Eros is 'a relation with alterity, with mystery, that is with the future, with that which is absent from the world that contains everything that is...' 'The pathos of love consists in the insurmountable duality of beings.' Attempts to overcome that duality, to tame the wayward and domesticate the riotous, to make the unknowable predictable and enchain the free-roaming – all such things sound the death-knell to love. Eros won't outlast duality. As

7

far as love is concerned, possession, power, fusion, and disenchant-
ment are the Four Horsemen of the Apocalypse.

In this lies the wondrous fragility of love, side by side with its
cursed refusal to bear vulnerability lightly. All love strives to
foreclose, but at the moment of triumph it meets its ultimate
defeat. All love struggles to bury the sources of its precariousness
and suspense; but if it succeeds, it quickly starts wilting – and
fades. Eros is possessed by the ghost of Thanatos which no
magic incantations can exorcise. This is not a matter of Eros's
precocity, and no amount of schooling and teach-yourself expedients can free it from the morbid – suicidal – inclination.

The challenge, the pull, the seduction of the Other render all
distance, however reduced and minuscule, unbearably large. The
opening feels like a precipice. Fusion or overpowering seem the
only cures for the resulting torment. And there is but a thin
boundary, all too easy to overlook, between a soft and gentle
caress and a ruthless iron grip. Eros cannot be loyal to itself
without practising the first, but cannot practise it without risking
the second. Eros prompts a hand to be stretched towards the other
– but hands that may caress may also clutch and squeeze.

**However much you have learned about love and loving, your
wisdom may only come, like Kafka's Messiah, a day after its
arrival.**

As long as it lives, love hovers on the brink of defeat. It dissolves
its past as it goes; it leaves no fortified trenches behind to which it
could retreat, running for shelter in case of trouble. And it knows
not what lies ahead and what the future may bring. It will never
gain confidence strong enough to disperse the clouds and stifle
anxiety. Love is a mortgage loan drawn on an uncertain, and
inscrutable, future.

Love may be, and often is, as frightening as death; only, unlike
death, it covers up that truth by the flurry of desire and excitement.
It makes sense to think of the difference between love and death as
one between attraction and repulsion. On second thoughts,
though, one cannot be that sure. Love's promises are as a rule
less ambiguous than its gifts. Thus the temptation to fall in love is

great and overwhelming, but so also is the attraction of escape. And the enticement to seek a rose without thorns is never far away and always difficult to resist.

Desire and love. Siblings. Sometimes born as twins; never, though, as identical (single egg) twins.

Desire is the wish to consume. To imbibe, devour, ingest and digest – annihilate. Desire needs no other prompt but the presence of alterity. That presence is always and already an affront and a humiliation. Desire is the urge to avenge the affront and avert the humiliation. It is a compulsion to close the gap to alterity, as it beckons and repels, as it seduces by the promise of the unexplored and irritates by its evasive, stubborn otherness. Desire is an impulse to strip alterity of its otherness; thereby, to disempower. From the tasting, exploring, familiarizing and domesticating, alterity would emerge with the sting of temptation pulled out and broken. If it survives the treatment, that is. The odds are, though, that in the process its undigested remnants will have fallen from the realm of consumables to that of waste.

Consumables attract; waste repels. After desire comes waste disposal. It is, it seems, the squeezing of alienness out of alterity *and* the dumping of the dessicated carapace that congeal into the joy of satisfaction, bound to dissipate as soon as the job is done. In its essence, desire is an urge of destruction. And, though but obliquely, the urge of *self*-destruction: desire is contaminated, from its birth, by the death-wish. This is, though, its closely guarded secret; guarded mostly from itself.

Love is, on the other hand, the wish to care, and to preserve the object of the care. A centrifugal impulse, unlike centripetal desire. An impulse to expand, to go beyond, to stretch to what is 'out there'. To ingest, absorb and assimilate the subject in the object, not vice versa as in the case of desire. Love is about adding to the world – each addition being the living trace of the loving self; in love, the self is, bit by bit, transplanted onto the world. *The loving self expands through giving itself away to the loved object.* Love is about self's survival-through-self's-alterity. And so love means an urge to protect, to feed, to shelter; also to caress, cosset and

9

pamper, or to jealously guard, fence off, incarcerate. Love means being-in-service, standing-in-disposition, awaiting command – but it may also mean expropriation and seizing of responsibility. Mastery through surrender; sacrifice rebounding as aggrandizement. Love is a Siamese twin of power greed; neither would survive the separation.

If desire wants to consume, love wants to possess. While the fulfilment of desire is coterminous with the annihilation of its object – love grows with its acquisitions and is fulfilled in their durability. If desire is self-destructive, love is self-perpetuating.

Like desire, love is a threat to its object. Desire destroys its object, destroying itself in the process; the protective net which love weaves caringly around its object love enslaves its object. Love takes captive and puts the apprehended in custody; it makes an arrest, for the prisoner's protection.

Desire and love act at cross-purposes. Love is a net cast on eternity, desire is a stratagem to be spared the chores of net weaving. True to their nature, love would strive to perpetuate the desire. Desire, on the other hand, would shun love's shackles.

'Your eyes meet across a crowded room; the spark of attraction is there. You chat, dance, laugh, share a drink or a joke, and before you know it, one of you asks: "Your place or mine?" None of you is on the lookout for anything serious, but somehow one night may turn into a week, then a month, a year, or longer' – notes Catherine Jarvie (in *Guardian Weekend*).[3]

Such an unanticipated outcome of the flash of desire and a one-night stand to quash it is, in Jarvie's expression, an 'emotional halfway house between the freedom of dating and the seriousness of a major relationship' (though 'seriousness', as she reminds her readers, does not protect a 'major relationship' from ending in 'difficulties and bitterness' when one partner 'remains committed to carrying on while the other is keen to hunt out pastures new'). Halfway houses – like all other admittedly 'until further notice' arrangements in a fluid setting in which binding the future is as hopeless as it is resented – are not necessarily a bad thing (in the opinion of Jarvie and Dr Valerie Lamont, a chartered counselling psychologist she quotes); but when 'committing yourself, however half-heartedly', 'remember that you are likely to be closing the door to other romantic possibilities' (that is, surrendering the right to 'hunting out pastures new', at least until the partner claims that right first).

A sharp observation, a sober assessment: you are in a trade-off situation. Desire and love are either/or.

More sharp observations: your eyes meet across the room, and before you know it . . . Desire to play in bed together leaps out of nowhere, and it does not need much knocking on the door to be let in. Perhaps uncharacteristically in our security-obsessed world these are doors with few if any locks. No closed-circuit TV to closely examine the intruders and set apart vicious prowlers from bona fide visitors. Checking the compatibility of zodiac signs (as in the television commercials of a mobile telephone brand) would do the trick.

Perhaps to say 'desire' is to say too much. As in shopping: shoppers these days do not buy to satisfy desire, as Harvie Ferguson observed – they buy *on wish*. It takes time (an unbearably lengthy time by the standards of a culture that abhors procrastination and promotes 'instant satisfaction' instead) to sow, cultivate and feed desire. Desire needs time to germinate, grow and mellow. As 'long term' shrinks shorter and shorter, still the speed of desire's ripening stubbornly resists acceleration; the time needed to cash in the returns on the investment in the cultivation of desire feels longer and longer – irritatingly and unaffordably long.

Managers of shopping malls have not been offered such time by their shareholders, but neither do they want to let shopping decisions be prompted by motives that are born and mature at random, or to abandon their cultivation to the inexpert and unreliable DIY exploits of the shoppers. All the motives needed to make shoppers shop must be born on the spot, while strolling the mall. They may also die on the spot (by an assisted suicide, in most cases) once their job has been done. Their life expectation need not stretch longer than it takes the shoppers to wander from the entry to the shopping mall to the exit.

11

These days, shopping malls tend to be designed with the fast arousal and quick extinction of wishes in mind, not the cumbersome and protracted breeding and grooming of desires. The sole desire that should (and would) be implanted by a visit to a shopping mall is that of repeating, over and over again, the exhilarating moment of 'letting oneself go' and allowing the wishes to run the show without a prescripted scenario. The brevity of their life expectation is the wishes' major asset, giving them an edge over desires. Surrendering to wishes, unlike following a desire, is known to be but momentary, bearing the hope that it will leave no lasting consequences that could bar further moments of joyful ecstasy. In the case of partnerships, and sexual partnerships in particular, following wishes rather than desires means leaving the door wide open 'to other romantic possibilities' that, as Dr Lamont suggests and Catherine Jarvie muses, may 'be more satisfying and fulfilling'.

With acting-on-wishes drilled deeply into daily conduct by the mighty powers of the consumer market, following a desire seems to steer uneasily, awkwardly, discomfortingly to loving commitment's side.

In its orthodox rendition, desire needs tending and grooming, involving protracted care, difficult bargaining with no foregone resolution, some hard choices and a few painful compromises – but worst of all entailing a delay of satisfaction, no doubt the sacrifice most abhorred in our world of speed and acceleration. In its radicalized, tapered and above all more compact reincarnation as a wish, desire has lost most of such off-putting attributes, while focusing more closely on its target. As the commercials heralding the introduction of credit cards famously put it – one may now 'take the waiting out of wanting'.

When guided by wish ('your eyes meet across a crowded room'), partnership follows the pattern of shopping and calls for nothing more than the skills of an average, moderately experienced consumer. Like other consumer goods, partnership is for consumption on-the-spot (it does not require additional training or prolonged preparation) and for one-off use 'without prejudice'. First and foremost, it is eminently disposable.

If found faulty or not 'fully satisfactory', goods may be exchanged for other, hopefully more satisfying commodities, even if an after-sales service is not offered and a money-back guarantee not included in the transaction. But even if they deliver on their promise, they are not expected to be in use for long; after all, perfectly usable, shipshape cars, or computers or mobile telephones in quite decent working condition are consigned to the rubbish heap with little or no regret the moment their 'new and improved versions' appear in the shops and become the talk of the town. Any reason why partnerships should be an exception to the rule?

Promises of commitment, writes Adrienne Burgess, 'are meaningless in the long term'.[4]

And she goes on to explain: 'Commitment is a spin-off from other things: how satisfied we are with our relationship; whether we see a viable alternative to it; and whether moving on would cause us to lose important investment (time, money, shared property, children).' But 'these factors wax and wane, as do people's feelings of commitment,' according to Caryl Rusbult, a 'relationship expert' at the University of North Carolina.

A quandary, indeed: you are reluctant to cut your losses, but you loathe the prospect of throwing good money after bad. A relationship, the expert will tell you, is an investment like all the others: you put in time, money, efforts that you could have turned to other aims but did not, hoping that you were doing the right thing and that what you've lost or refrained from otherwise enjoying would be in due course repaid – with profit. You buy stocks and hold them as long as they promise to grow in value, and promptly sell them when the profits begin to fall or when other stocks promise a higher income (the trick is not to overlook the moment when that happens). If you invest in a relationship, the profit you expect is first and foremost security: security in its many senses – of the nearness of a helping hand when you need it most, of succour in grief, of company in loneliness, of bailing out in trouble, of consolation in defeat and applause in victory; also in the sense of gratification that promptly arrives in the wake of a need. But be warned: promises of commitment to the relationship, once it is entered, are 'meaningless in the long term'.

Of course they are; relationships are investments like any other, but would it ever occur to you to take an oath of loyalty to the stocks you have just bought from the broker? To swear that you'd remain *semper fidelis* through thick and thin, for richer and poorer, 'till death us do part'? Never to look sideways, where (who knows?) greater prizes may beckon?

Stockholders worth their salt (pay attention: stockholders only *hold* the stocks, and what you hold, you may let go) open the newspaper stock-exchange pages first thing in the morning to find out whether it is time to hold on or to let go. And so with that other kind of stock: relationships. Only in this case no stock exchanges operate and no one will do the job of weighing the probabilities and evaluating the chances for you (unless you hire an expert counsellor, in the same way as you hire a stock-exchange adviser or a chartered accountant, though in the case of relationships innumerable chat shows and 'true life dramas' try hard to fill the expert's place). And so you have to do it, day in day out, on your own. If you make a mistake, you'll be denied the comfort of blaming wrong information. You must be constantly on the alert. Woe to you if you take a nap or let your vigilance slip. 'Being in a relationship' means a lot of headaches, but above all perpetual uncertainty. You can never be really, fully sure what to do – and never certain that you have done the right thing or that you did it at the right time.

It looks as if the quandary has no good solution. Worse still, it seems that it is pregnant with a paradox of the most invidious sort: not just that the relationship fails to gratify the need it was meant (and hoped) to placate, but that it makes that need yet more vexatious and trying. You sought the relationship in the hope of mitigating the insecurity that haunted your loneliness; but the therapy has all but inflamed the symptoms, and now you feel perhaps even less secure than before, even if the 'new and aggravated' insecurity oozes from different quarters. If you thought that the interest on your investment in company would be paid in the hard currency of security, you seem to have acted on wrong assumptions.

This is trouble and nothing but trouble, but not the whole trouble. A commitment to a relationship that is 'meaningless in the long term' (of which *both* sides are aware!) is a two-edged sword. It makes the holding or the forfeiting of the investment a matter of your calculation and decision – but there is no reason to suppose that your partner won't wish, if need be, to exercise a similar discretion and won't be free to do so if and when she or he wishes. Your awareness of this adds yet more to your uncertainty – and the bit it has added is the most difficult to endure: unlike in the case of your own 'keep it or leave it' choice, it is not in your power to prevent your partner from opting out from the deal. You can do pretty little to change the partner's decision in your favour. For your partner, you are the stock to be sold or the loss to be cut – and no one consults the stocks before sending them back to the market, or the losses before cutting them out.

By all accounts, relationship seen as a business transaction is not a cure for insomnia. Investment in the relationship is unsafe and bound to remain unsafe even if you wish otherwise: a headache, not a medicine. As long as relationships are viewed as profitable investments, as warrants of security and resolutions to your problems, it seems that heads the other wins and tails you lose. Loneliness spawns insecurity – but relationship seems to do nothing else. In a relationship, you may feel as insecure as without it, or worse. Only the names you give your anxiety change.

If there is no good solution to a quandary, if none of the allegedly sensible and effective steps brings the solution any closer – people tend to behave irrationally, adding to the problem and making its resolution even less plausible.

As another relationship expert quoted by Adrienne Burgess, Christopher Clulow of the Tavistock Marital Studies Institute, concludes – 'When lovers feel insecure, they tend to behave unconstructively, either trying to please or trying to control, perhaps even lashing out physically – all are likely to drive the lover away.' Once insecurity creeps in, navigation is never confident, thoughtful and steady. Rudderless, the frail raft of relationship sways between one and the other of the two ill-famed rocks on which many a partnership flounders: total submission and total power, meek acceptance and arrogant conquest, effacing one's own autonomy and stifling the autonomy of the partner. Hitting either of the two rocks would wreck even a shipshape boat with a seasoned crew – let alone a raft carrying an inexperienced sailor who, having been brought up in the spare-parts era, never had a chance to learn the art of damage repair. None of the up-to-date sailors would waste time on repairing the part that is no longer seaworthy and would rather put a spare in its place. But on the raft of relationship, spares are not available.

Failure of a relationship is more often than not a failure of communication.

As Knud Løgstrup – first the soft-spoken evangelist from the parish of Funen and later the clarion-voiced ethical philosopher of the University of Aarhus – observed, there are 'two divergent perversions' waiting in ambush for the unwary or unthinking communicator.[5] One is 'the kind of association which, due to laziness, fear of people, or a propensity for cosy relationships, consists in simply trying to please one another while always dodging the issue. With the possible exception of a common cause against a third person, there is nothing which promotes a comfortable relationship quite so much as mutual praise.' Another perversion consists in 'our wanting to change other people. We have definite opinions about how to do things and how others ought to be. These opinions are lacking in understanding, because the more definitive the opinions are, the more necessary it becomes that we are not distracted by too much understanding of those who are to be changed.'

The trouble is that both perversions are all too often the children of love. The first perversion may be the outcome of my desire for comfort and peace, as Løgstrup implies. But it may also be, and often is, a product of my loving respect for the other: I love you, and so I let you be as you are and insist on being, whatever doubts I may have as to the wisdom of your choice. Whatever harm your

16

obstinacy may cause you, I would not dare to contradict you, lest you be forced to make a choice between your freedom and my love. You can count on my approval, whatever happens...And since love cannot but be possessive, my loving generosity is hope-assisted: that blank cheque is a gift of my love, a precious gift not found elsewhere. My love is that tranquil haven which you sought and which you needed even if you did not seek it. You may now rest and seek it no longer...

This is love's possessiveness at work; but a possessiveness that seeks its fulfilment through self-restraint.

The second perversion stems from love's possessiveness let loose and on the rampage. Love is one of the palliative answers to the blessing/curse of human individuality, one of whose many attributes is the loneliness with which the condition of separation is bound to be pregnant (as Erich Fromm suggests,[6] humans of all ages and cultures are confronted with the solution of one and the same question: the question of how to overcome separateness, how to achieve union, how to transcend one's own individual life and find 'at-onement'). All love is tinged with the anthropophagic urge. All lovers want to smother, extirpate and cleanse the vexing, irritating alterity that separates them from the beloved; separation from the beloved is the lover's most gruesome fear, and many a lover would go to any lengths to stave off the spectre of leave-taking once and for all. What better way of reaching that goal than making the beloved an undetachable part of the lover? Wherever I go, you go; whatever I do, you do; whatever I accept, you accept; whatever I resent, you resent. If you are not and cannot be my Siamese twin, be my clone!

The second perversion has another root as well – and it is sunk in the lover's adoration of the beloved. In their introduction to a collection of texts under the title *Philosophies of Love*,[7] David L. Norton and Mary F. Kille tell the story of a man who invited friends to dinner to meet 'the perfect incarnation of Beauty, Virtue, Wisdom, and Grace, in short, the loveliest woman in the world'; later the same day, at the restaurant table, the invited friends 'struggled to conceal their astonishment': was this 'the creature whose beauty outshines Venus, Helen, and Lady Hamilton?' It is

17

sometimes difficult to tell the adoration of the beloved from self-adoration; one can spy a trace of an expansive yet insecure ego desperate to confirm its uncertain merits through its looking-glass reflection, or better still in a flattering, laboriously retouched portrait. Is it not true that some of my unique valour has rubbed off onto the person that *I* (remember: *I*, myself, exercising my sovereign will and discretion) have chosen – one I have picked from the crowds of the anonymous and the ordinary to be my – *mine* only – companion? In the dazzling shine of the chosen, my own incandescence finds its glowing reflection. It adds to my glory, it confirms my glory and endorses it, it carries the news and the proofs of my glory wherever it goes.

But can I be sure? I would be, were there no doubts rattling in that dark dungeon of the unthought where I locked them in the vain hope of never hearing from them again. Qualms, misgivings; apprehensions that the virtue might be flawed, the glory fanciful... that the distance between me as I am and the real me that craves to come out but so far has not still needs to be negotiated – and doing that is a tall order.

My beloved could be a billboard on which my perfection is painted in all its magnificence and splendour; but would not stains and smudges show as well? To wipe them clean, or to hide them in case they are too sticky to be rubbed out, one needs to thoroughly cleanse and then prime the canvas before the painting job starts in earnest; and then watch carefully to make sure the traces of the old imperfections don't come out of hiding from under successive layers of paint. Each moment of rest is a moment too early – restoration and repainting without respite...

That never-ending effort is *also* a labour of love. Love is bursting with creative energy; time and again the energy is released in an outburst or a steady flow of destruction.

In the process, the beloved has turned into a canvas. Blank canvas, preferably. Its natural colours have been blanched, so as not to jar with, or disfigure, the painter's likeness. The painter need not inquire how the canvas feels, down there, underneath all that paint. Canvas canvases or linen canvases do not volunteer reports. Though human canvases do, on occasion.

It may be love in a flash, love at first sight; but time, long or short, must elapse between the question and the answer, the proposal and its acceptance.

The time that elapses is never so short as to allow the one who asked and the one who answered to remain, at the moment the answer arrives, the same beings they were when the clock was set: the one who asked and the one who was asked. As Franz Rosenzweig put it, 'the answer is unavoidably given by another person than the one who was asked, and it is given to one who has changed since he asked it. It is impossible to know how profound the change has been.'[8] Asking the question, waiting for an answer, being asked a question, struggling with the answer, is what made the change.

Both partners knew that the change was coming and both welcomed it. They jumped headlong into the uncharted waters; the chance to open themselves up to the adventure of the unknown and the unpredictable was love's greatest seduction. 'The first relief from tension in the enchanted game of love usually comes when the lovers call each other by their first names. This act stands as a solitary pledge that the yesterdays of the two individuals will be incorporated in their today.' And – let me add – readiness to incorporate shared tomorrows into their half-shared, half-separate, individual todays. The tomorrow that follows that incorporation will – will have to – differ from today, as it differs from the yesterdays. John will be John *and* Mary, Mary will be Mary *and* John.

Odo Marquard spoke, not necessarily tongue in cheek, about the etymological kinship between *zwei* and *Zweifel* – 'two' and 'doubt' – and suggested that there is more to that link than mere alliteration. When there are two, there is no certainty; and when the other is recognized as the fully fledged 'second', a *sovereign* second, not a mere extension, or an echo, or a tool, or an orderly of me *the first* – the uncertainty is acknowledged and accepted. Being twosome means consent to undetermined future.

Franz Kafka observed that we are doubly separated from God. Having eaten from the tree of knowledge we have separated *us from Him* – while the fact that we have not eaten from the tree of life separates *Him from us*. Him (eternity, in which all beings and their deeds are embraced; in which whatever may be, is, and whatever may happen, does) is closed to us; bound to stay secret – forever beyond comprehension. But we know that – and this knowledge allows us no rest. Starting with the failed attempt to build the Tower of Babel, we cannot stop trying and erring and failing and trying again.

Trying what? To deny that separation, to deny the denial of right to the tree of life's fruits. Going on trying and failing the trials is human, all too human. If alterity is, as Levinas insists, the ultimate mystery, the absolutely unknown and the utterly impenetrable, it cannot but be an offence and a challenge – precisely for being divine: barring access, denying entry, unattainable and forever beyond reach. But (as Rosenzweig keeps reminding us), 'the un-limited cannot be attained by organization . . . The highest things cannot be planned; for them readiness is everything.'

Readiness for what? 'Speech is bound by time and nourished by time . . . It does not know in advance just where it will end. It takes its cue from others. In fact, it lives by virtue of another's life . . . In actual conversation something happens.' Rosenzweig explains who that 'another' is, by whose life speech lives so that something may happen in the conversation: that 'another' 'is always a quite definite someone' who has 'not merely ears, like "all the world", but also a mouth'.

This is exactly what love does: wrenching *an* other from 'all the world', and through that act remoulding 'an' other into the 'quite *definite* someone', someone with a mouth to listen to, someone with whom to converse so that something may happen.

And what is that 'something' to be? Love means suspending the answer, or refraining from asking the question. Making *an* other into the *definite* someone means rendering the future indefinite. It means consent to the future's indefiniteness. Consent to a life lived, from its conception to its demise, on the only site allocated to humans: the void stretching between finitude of their deeds and infinity of their aims and consequences.

'Top-pocket relationship', explains Catherine Jarvie, commenting on the opinions of Gillian Walton of London Marriage Guidance,[9] is so called because you keep it in your pocket so that you can bring it out when you need it.

A successful top-pocket relationship is sweet and short-lived, says Jarvie. We may suppose that it is sweet *because* it is short-lived, and that its sweetness dwells precisely in that comforting awareness that you do not need to go out of your way or stretch yourself over backwards to keep its sweetness intact for a longer time; in fact, you need not do anything at all to enjoy it. 'Top-pocket relationship' is instantaneity and disposability incarnate.

Not that your relationship would acquire those wondrous qualities without certain conditions having first been met. Note that it is *you* who must meet those conditions; another point in the 'top-pocket' relationship's favour, to be sure, since it is on you and only you that success depends, and so it is you and only you who is in control – and stays in control throughout the 'top-pocket' relationship's short life.

First condition: the relationship must be entered in full awareness and soberly. No 'love at first sight' here, remember. No *falling* in love ... No sudden tide of emotions that leave you breathless and gasping: neither the emotions we call 'love', nor those we soberly describe as 'desire'. Don't let yourself be overwhelmed and shaken off your feet, and above all don't let your calculator be torn out of your hand. And don't allow yourself to mistake what the relationship you are about to enter is about, for what it neither is nor should be about. Convenience is the sole thing that counts, and convenience is a matter for a clear head, not a warm (let alone overheated) heart. The smaller your mortgage loan, the less insecure you'd feel when exposed to the fluctuations of the future housing market; the less you invest in the relationship, the less insecure you'd feel when exposed to the fluctuations of your future emotions.

Second condition: keep it this way. Remember that convenience needs little time to turn into its opposite. So don't let the relationship escape from the head's supervision, don't allow it to develop its own logic and particularly to acquire rights of tenure – to fall out of your top pocket where it belongs. Be on the alert. Don't let your vigilance take a nap. Watch closely even the slightest changes

21

in what Jarvie calls 'emotional undercurrents' (obviously, emotions tend to become 'undercurrents' once they have been left out of the calculation). If you note something that you did not bargain for and would not care for – know that 'it's time to move on'. Travelling cautiously would spare you the ennui of arrival. It is the traffic that holds all the pleasure.

So keep your top pocket free and ready. You will soon need to put something there, and – keep your fingers crossed – you will . . .

The 'Relationships spirit' section of the _Guardian Weekend_ is worth reading every week, but it is even better to read it many weeks in a row.

Each week it offers advice on how to proceed when confronting a 'problem' most men and women (mainly _Guardian_ readers) are expected, and so duly expect, sooner or later to confront. One week, one problem; but over a succession of weeks the dedicated and attentive reader can gain much more than certain specific life-political skills that may come in handy in certain specific situations in tackling certain specific problems; skills that, once acquired and combined, could help to _create_ the kinds of situations they have been conceived to deal with and to spot and locate the problems they have been designed to tackle. A regular and dedicated reader blessed with a longer memory-span than a single week can draw and fill in a complete map of the life in which 'problems' tend to crop up, register the complete inventory of 'problems' that do, and form an opinion of their relative frequency or rarity. In a world where the gravity of a thing or an event is represented only in numbers, and so can only be grasped that way (the quality of a hit in the number of sold records, of a public event or performance in the number of TV watchers, of a public figure in the number of people passing by the coffin, of the intellectuals in public view in the numbers of quotes and mentions), the high frequency with which some 'problems' keep returning to the column, in various guises, week after week after week, is all the testimony one needs to their relevance to a successful life, and so to the importance of the skills designed to tackle them.

22

So, when it comes to the relationships as seen through the prism of the 'Relationships spirit' column, what can a faithful reader learn about the relative importance of things and the techniques of handling them?

The reader may learn quite a few useful hints about the places where would-be relationship partners can be found in larger than usual quantities, and about the situations in which, once found, they are more likely to be prevailed upon or cajoled to assume the partner's role. And he or she would know that entering a relationship is a 'problem'; that is, it presents a difficulty which spawns confusion and brings about unpleasant tension which, in order to be fought against and chased away, needs a certain amount of knowing and know-how. This would be learnt – without swotting, just by following regularly, week by week, the *Guardian Weekend* version of the relationship spirit.

This won't be, however, the main lesson likely to trickle down and take root in the regular reader's vision of life and life politics. The art of *breaking up* the relationship and emerging out of it unscathed, with few if any festering wounds needing a lot of time to heal and a lot of care to limit the 'collateral damage' (like estranged friends, or circles where one would not be welcomed or which one would wish to avoid), beats the art of *composing* relationships hands down – by the sheer frequency of being vented.

It seems that Richard Baxter, the fiery Puritan prophet, were he instead a prophet of life strategy fit for the liquid modern era, would say of relationships what he did of the acquisition and care of external goods – that they 'should only lie on the shoulders like a light cloak, which can be thrown aside at any moment', and that one should beware more than anything else their turning, unintentionally and surreptitiously, into 'a steel casing'... You won't take your riches with you to the grave, the prophet-saint Baxter admonished his flock, rehearsing the common sense of the people who lived their life as handmaiden of the afterlife. You won't take your relations into the next episode, the expert-counsellor Baxter would admonish his clients, in unison with the premonitions-turned-certainties of the wise-after-the-fact people whose lives have been sliced into episodes lived through as handmaidens of the episodes yet to come. Your relationship is likely to break up well before the episode ends. But if it doesn't, there will hardly be another episode. Certainly not another episode to savour and enjoy.

The astounding ratings success of *EastEnders* conveys an apparently different message...

The enchanted/addicted audience goes from strength to strength, and so does the self-confidence of the scriptwriters, producers and actors. That soap opera seems to have hit a target that other soaps have overlooked or tried to reach in vain and kept missing. What is its secret?

Most relationships that the *EastEnders* characters *enter* look as frail as any others known to the viewers from frustrations experienced first-hand or the cautionary tales of other people's frustrations (including the messages that keep coming from the 'Relationship spirit' column). Hardly any of the bonds tied by the *EastEnders* characters has survived the smooth flow of the episodes for more than a few months – sometimes only weeks – and among the deceased relationships those ended by 'natural causes' have been few and far between. A viewer with long memory would see the Square as a graveyard of human relationships...

Entering relations *EastEnders* style is anything but easy. It takes effort and calls for considerable skills, which many hapless characters lack and only a handful have been born with (though sometimes it also needs a stroke of luck, notorious for being sparsely and haphazardly distributed). The troubles do not end when the couple moves in together. Shared rooms may be sites of many joyful revelries but seldom of safety and restfulness. Some are stages for cruel dramas, complete with verbal skirmishes escalating to fisticuffs and (if the couple does not split before it comes to that) developing eventually into full-scale hostilities heading to a denouement just a few steps away from *Reservoir Dogs*. Elaborate wedding ceremonies do not help; stag and hen nights do not bring an end to the risk-fraught and accident-prone Unknown, and wedding days are not new beginnings ushering the couple into 'something completely different' – they are just short breaks in a drama without scenario and scripted lines.

Partnership is but a coalition of 'confluent interests', and in the fluid world of *EastEnders* people come and go, opportunities knock and disappear again shortly after being let in, fortunes rise and fall and coalitions tend to be floating, flexible and frail. People seek partners and 'enter relationships' in order to escape the vexation of frailty, only to find that frailty yet more vexing and painful than before. What was meant/hoped/expected to be a shelter (perhaps *the* shelter) against fragility proves time and again to be its hothouse ...

Millions of *EastEnders* fans and addicts watch and nod. Yes, we know all that, we have seen all that, we have lived through all that. What we have learned the hard way is that the state of having been abandoned to one's own company, and with no one to count on to stroke, console and give a hand, is dreadful and scary, but that one never feels more alone and abandoned than when struggling to make sure that there is indeed someone today who can also be counted on tomorrow and the day after tomorrow to do all that if – when – the wheel of fortune turns the other way. The outcomes of your struggle are impossible to predict – and the struggle itself takes its toll. Sacrifices are demanded daily. There is hardly a day without a tiff or a fisticuff. Waiting until the goodness hiding (as you keenly wish to believe and so do passionately believe) deep inside your chosen partner breaks through the evil carapace and reveals itself may take much longer than you can endure. And there is a lot of pain felt, and tears shed, and blood spilt, while you are waiting ...

EastEnders episodes are three-a-week rehearsals of day-to-day life wisdom. Regular, reliable reassurances for the unsure: yes, this is your life, and the truth of life of the others like you. Don't panic, take it as it comes, and don't forget for a moment that come it will – you can be sure it will. No one says that *making* people into your partners-in-fate is easy; but there is no other way but to try, and try, and try again.

This is not the only message, though, that *EastEnders* brings home three times a week and thanks to which it has become and remains such compelling viewing for so many. There is another message as well. In case you forget, there is a second line of trenches in that unending life battle; a ready-made, last ditch defence against the caprices of erratic fortune and the surprises that the poker-faced world holds up its sleeve. The trenches have already been dug for you before you've started digging your own; the trenches are waiting for you just to jump in. No one is going to ask questions, no one will inquire what you have done to earn the right to ask for succour and help. Whatever you've done, no one will refuse you entry.

There are Butchers, Mitchells, Slaters. Clans you happen to belong to without ever joining or asking admission. You need do nothing at all to *become* 'one of them'. Though you can do pretty little to *stop* being one of them. They would promptly remind you, if you were to forget those simple truths.

And so you find yourself in a double bind. Unless you are one of those few exceptionally unscrupulous, unruly, adventurous or psychotic miscreants and 'natural' outcasts who would soon be bound to have to go into hiding, be run over by a car, be chased away by neighbours, be locked in prison – or use other tested outlets to vanish from Albert Square – you would want to use both the anchors life gave you to moor in the company of others. You would wish to hold onto the partner of *your choice* and to the clan that has been *chosen for you* by fate.

That may not be easy, though – like enjoying the warmth of a fireplace and the pleasures of a swim in the sea at the same time. The meanderings of the Albert Square characters amply and graphically depict all the obstacles that pile up on your way; this is another reason to watch their exploits three times a week. You see what you've felt all along: you are the sole link connecting the partner you love and wish to be loved by, with the family clan that you belong to, that you wish to belong to and that wishes you to belong to it and to obey it. And so you are indeed 'the weakest link' – one who suffers most of the strain the tug-of-war between the two sides causes.

The perpetually simmering and occasionally seething war of attrition whose first victims are those who dream of reconciliation came to its dramatic climax – indeed, rose to the heights of Antigone's tragedy – in Little Mo's trial, the updated version of Sophocles' immortal play and the immortal story that play recorded...

Says Antigone: 'O but I would not have done the forbidden thing/ For any husband or for any son./For why? I could have had another husband/and by him other sons, if one were lost;/but, father and mother lost, where would I get/another brother?' Losing a husband is not the end of the road. Husbands, even in ancient Greece (though not as much as for the contemporaries of Little Mo), are but temporary; losing them is painful no doubt, yet *curable*. Loss of parents is, on the contrary, *irrevocable*. Is this enough for duty to the family to override the debt to the husband? Perhaps such a sober calculation would not suffice, were it not for another reason: demands coming from a *chosen* companion, a temporary and in principle replaceable fellow-traveller through life, carry less weight than those other demands heard from the depth of the bottomless, inscrutable past: 'That order did not come from God. Justice that dwells with the gods below, knows no such law./I did not think your edicts strong enough/ to overrule the unwritten unalterable laws / of God and heaven, you being only a man./They are not of yesterday or to-day, but everlasting,/though where they came from, none of us can tell.'

Here, you would say, Little Mo and Antigone part ways. Indeed, one can hardly hear the residents of Albert Square mentioning God (the few who do, quickly disappear from the soap saga, as blatantly out of place). In that Square, as in so many other squares and streets of our towns, *Deus* has been for a very long time *absconditus*, He carries no mobile and keeps its number ex-directory, and so no one can credibly claim to know exactly what His instructions would sound like if they were audible. The rights of the family may be longer lasting than the duty toward the chosen partner, but in Albert Square neither seems to carry a Divine sanction. Little Mo's sorry predicament does not arise from the fear of God. So in what way, if any, is Little Mo's drama a rehearsal of Antigone's tragedy?

In Sophocles' version of Antigone's story, the Messenger enters the stage to sum up the tale's meaning, but also to anticipate, and answer, our question, a question that unlike the words used to make it legible to the viewers obviously did not – does not – age: 'What is the life of man? A thing not fixed/for good or evil, fashioned for praise or blame. Chance raises a man to the heights, chance casts him down,/ and none can foretell what will be from what is.'

So it is *the future*, the frighteningly unknown and impenetrable future (that is, as Levinas insisted, the epitome, the paragon, the fullest incarnation of 'absolute alterity'), and not the dignity of however venerable a past, that lurks behind the dilemma confronted by Little Mo as much as by Antigone. 'None can foretell what will be from what is' – but none can bear that impossibility lightly. In the sea of uncertainty, one seeks salvation on little islands of safety. Is something that boasts a longer past more likely to enter the future uninjured and unscathed than something else, admittedly 'man-made, man-unmade', blatantly 'of yesterday or of today'? There is no knowing, but it is tempting to think that it is. Little to choose from, anyway, in that endless, forever unfinished and frustrating, search for certainty...

Having heard the adverse verdict of the jury, it is to her Dad that Little Mo addresses her 'I am sorry'...

In the German language, affinity is the marked member in opposition to kinship.

'Affinity' is kinship *qualified* – kinship *but*...(*Wahl verwandschaft*, wrongly and misleadingly translated into English as 'elective affinity', a blatant pleonasm, since no *affinity* can be non-elective; only *kinship* is, purely and simply, want it or not, *given*...). Choice is the qualifying factor: it transforms kinship into affinity. It also, however, betrays affinity's ambition: its intention to be *like* kinship, as unconditional, irrevocable and unbreakable as kinship is (eventually, affinity will weave into the lineage and become indistinguishable from the rest of the kinship network; the affinity of one generation will turn into the kinship of the next). But even marriages, contrary to priestly insistence, are not made in heaven – and what has been tied together by humans, humans may, and can, and given a chance will untie.

28

One would dearly like to precede kinship with choice, but one would wish the aftermath of choice to be exactly what kinship already is: indomitably tough, durable, reliable, lasting, unbreakable. This is the ambivalence endemic to all *Wahlverwandschaft* – its birthmark (blight and charm; blessing and bane) that cannot be erased. The founding act of choice is affinity's seductive power *and* its damnation. The memory of choice, its original sin, is bound to cast a long shadow and darken even the brightest togetherness called 'affinity': choice, unlike the fate of kinship, is a two-way street. One can always turn back, and the knowledge of such a possibility makes the task of keeping direction all the more daunting.

Affinity is born of choice and the umbilical cord is never cut. Unless the choice is restated daily and ever new actions are taken to confirm it, affinity will wilt, fade and decay until it falls or crawls apart. The intention of keeping affinity alive and well portends a daily struggle and promises no rest to vigilance. For us, the denizens of the liquid modern world that abhors everything that is solid and durable, that is unfit for instant use and allows no end to effort, such a prospect may be more than one would willingly bargain for. Establishing a bond of affinity proclaims the intention of making the bond like that of kinship – but also the readiness to pay the price of the avatar in the hard currency of day-in, day-out drudgery. When the willingness (or, given the training offered and received, solvency of assets) is missing, one would be inclined to think twice before acting on the intention.

Hence living together ('and let us wait and see how *it* works and where it will lead to') acquires the attraction which the bonds of affinity lack. Its intentions are modest, oaths are not taken and declarations, if made, are not solemn, no strings are attached and no hands tied. More often than not, there is no congregation to bear witness and no plenipotentiary from on high to consecrate the union. You ask less, you settle for less, and so there is less mortgage to repay and the length of repayment is less daunting. Over 'living together', future kinship, whether desired or feared, does not cast its dark shadow. 'Living together' is *because of*, not *in*

29

order to. All options stay open, past deeds are not allowed to cut them back.

Bridges are useless unless they span the whole distance between the shores – but in 'living together' the other shore is wrapped in a mist that never dissolves, a mist no one wishes to dissolve and no one tries to blow away and disperse. There is no knowing what one will see when (if) the fog dissipates – and there is no knowing whether there is anything at all hiding in the fog. Is the other shore there, or is it but a *fata morgana*, an illusion conjured up by the fog, a figment of the imagination that makes you see bizarre shapes in the passing clouds?

Living together may mean sharing the boat, the mess-table and the sleeping berths. It may mean sailing together and sharing the joys and hardships of the voyage. But it is not about passing from one shore to another, and so its purpose is not to deputize for the (absent) solid bridges. A log of past adventures may be kept, but there is only a perfunctory mention in it of the itinerary and of the port of destination. The fog covering the other – unknown, un-mapped – shore may thin out and blow away, the contours of a port may emerge, a decision to harbour may be taken, but all this is not, nor is it meant to be, written down in the sailing papers.

Affinity is a bridge leading to the safe haven of kinship. Living together is neither such a bridge nor a labour of bridge-building. The togetherness of 'living together' and the togetherness of kin are two different universes with separate time-spaces, each complete with laws and logics of their own. No passage from one to the other is mapped in advance – though one may, by chance, run up against or bounce upon one. There is no knowing, at least not in advance, whether living together will turn out to be a thorough-fare or a cul-de-sac. The point is to walk through the days as if that difference did not matter, and so in a fashion that makes the issue of 'what is what' irrelevant.

The falling out of fashion and out of practice of orthodox affinity cannot but rebound on the plight of kinship. Lacking stable bridges for inflowing traffic, kinship networks feel frail and threatened. Their boundaries are blurred and disputed, they dissolve in a terrain with no clear-cut property titles and hereditary tenures – a frontier-land; sometimes a battlefield, other times an object of court battles that are no less bitter. Kinship networks cannot be sure of their chances of survival, let alone calculate their life expectations. That brittleness makes them all the more precious. They are now frail, subtle, delicate; they prompt protective feelings; they make one wish to hug, caress and cajole; they yearn to be treated with loving care. And they are no longer arrogant and cocky the way they used to be when our ancestors fulminated and rebelled against the toughness and stiffness of the family embrace. They are no longer sure of themselves, being instead painfully aware of how fatal for their survival a single false step might be. Blinkers and earplugs are no longer in use – families look and listen attentively, all too willing to correct their ways, and ready to repay care and love in the same currency.

Paradoxically, or not quite paradoxically after all, the pulling and holding powers of kin shoot up, as the magnetism and carrying power of affinity dwindle...

So here we are, vacillating and uneasily manoeuvring between the two worlds notoriously distanced from and at odds with each other, yet both desirable and desired – with no clearly plotted passages, let alone beaten tracks between them.

Thirty years ago (in *The Fall of Public Man*) Richard Sennett noted the advent of 'an ideology of intimacy' that 'transmutes political categories into psychological categories'.[10]

One particularly portentous outcome of that new ideology was the substitution of 'shared identity' for 'shared interests'. Identity-based fraternity was to become – so Sennett warned – an 'empathy for a select group of people allied with rejection of those not within the local circle'. 'Outsiders, unknowns, unlikes become creatures to be shunned.'

A few years later Benedict Anderson coined the term 'imagined community' to account for the mystery of self-identification with a large category of unknown strangers with whom one believes oneself to share something important enough to make one speak of them as 'we' of which I, the speaker, am a part. The fact that Anderson viewed such identification with a dispersed population

31

of unknown people as a mystery calling for explanation was an oblique confirmation – indeed, a tribute – to Sennett's hunches. By the time Anderson developed his model of 'imagined community', the disintegration of impersonal ties and bonds (and with them, as Sennett would point out, the art of 'civility' – of 'wearing the mask' that simultaneously protects and allows company to be enjoyed) had reached an advanced stage and so the rubbing and patting of shoulders, closeness, intimacy, 'sincerity', 'turning oneself inside out', holding no secrets, compulsive and compulsory confessing were fast becoming the sole human defences against loneliness and the sole yarn available to weave the craved-for togetherness. One could conceive of totalities larger than the mutual confession circle only as a 'we' swelled and stretched; as the sameness, misnamed 'identity', writ large. The only way to include the 'unknowns' into a 'we' was to cast them as would-be partners in confessional rituals, bound to reveal a similar (and so familiar) 'inside' once pressed to share their intimate sincerities.

The communion of inner selves grounded in mutually encouraged self-disclosures may be the nucleus of the love relationship. It may strike roots, germinate, thrive inside the self-sustained, or nearly self-sustained, island of shared biographies. But just like the moral party of two – which, whenever expanded to include a Third, and so set eye-to-eye with the 'public sphere', finds its moral intuitions and impulses insufficient to confront and to tackle the issues of impersonal justice which that public sphere spawns – the communion of love is caught by the outside world unprepared, not ready to cope, ignorant of the skills which coping would require.

Inside a love communion it is only natural to view friction and disagreement as a temporary irritant that will soon go away; but also to view them as a call to a remedial action that will prompt them to go. A perfect blend of selves seems a realistic prospect there, given enough patience and dedication – the qualities that love is confident of supplying in profusion. Even if the spiritual sameness of lovers is still some way ahead, it surely is not an idle dream or a fanciful illusion. It certainly can be reached – and it can be reached with resources already at the lovers', in their capacity as lovers, disposal.

But try to stretch the legitimate expectations of love far enough to tame, domesticate and detoxicate the mind-boggling medley of sounds and sights that fills the world beyond the island of love ... Then and there, the tested and trusted stratagems of love won't be of much help. On the island of love, agreement, understanding and the dreamed-of oneness-in-two may never be beyond reach, but this is not true for that infinite world outside (unless transmuted, by a magic wand, into Jürgen Habermas's consensus-seeking colloquium). The tools of I-Thou togetherness, however perfectly mastered and impeccably wielded, will prove helpless in the face of the variance, disparity and discord that separate the multitudes of those that are a potential 'Thou' from each other and keep them on a war footing: in a shooting, rather than talking, mood. Mastery of quite different techniques is called for when disagreement is a transient discomfort soon to be dissipated, and when discord (signalling the determination to self-assert) is here to stay for an indefinite time. The hope of consent draws people together and spurs them to more effort. Disbelief in unity, feeding and fed by the blatant inadequacy of the tools in hand, goads people away from each other and prompts an urge to escape.

The first consequence of rising disbelief in the likelihood of unity is the division of the map of the *Lebenswelt*, the lifeworld, into two continents largely incommunicado with each other. One is where consensus is sought at all cost (though mostly, perhaps all the time, with the skills acquired and learned in the shelter of intimacy) – but above all is presumed to be already 'there', predetermined by shared identity, waiting to be awakened and to reassert itself. And the other is where hope of spiritual unity, and so also any effort to uncover it or to build it from scratch, has been *a priori* abandoned so that the only exchange adumbrated is that of missiles, not words.

These days, however, that duality of *postures* (theorized for private use as the division of *humankind*) seems to be gradually receding into the background of daily life – together with the spatial dimensions of human proximity and distance. Just as up there in the vast expanses of the global frontier-land, so at grass-roots level, in the domain of life politics, the setting for action is a container filled with potential friends and enemies, in which floating coalitions and drifting enmities are expected to coalesce for a time, only to dissolve once more and make room for other and different condensations. The 'communities of *sameness*', pre-determined but waiting to be revealed and filled with substance, are giving way to 'communities of *occasion*', expected to self-compose around events, idols, panics or fashions: most diverse as focal points, yet sharing the trait of short, and shortening, life expectation. They last no longer than the emotions that keep them in the focus of attention and prompt the pooling of interests – fleeting, but no less intense for that – banding together and adhering 'to the cause'.

All that coming together and drifting apart makes it possible to follow simultaneously the drive for freedom and the craving for belonging – and to cover up, if not fully make up for, the short-changing of both yearnings.

Both urges melt and mix in the all-absorbing and all-consuming labour of 'networking' and 'surfing the network'. The ideal of 'connectedness' struggles to grasp the difficult, vexing dialectics of the two irreconcilables. It promises a safe (or non-fatal at least) navigation between the reefs of loneliness and commitment, the scourge of exclusion and the iron grip of bonds too tight, an irreparable detachment and irrevocable attachment.

We chat and we have 'buddies' to chat with. Buddies, as every chat addict knows, come and go, switch in and out – but there are always a few of them on the line itching to drown silence in 'messages'. In the 'buddy-buddy' sort of relationship, not messages as such, but the coming and going of messages, the *circulation* of messages, *are the message* – don't mind the content. We belong – to the even flow of words and unfinished sentences (abbreviated, to be sure, truncated to speed up the circulation). We belong to talking, not to what is talked *about*.

Don't confuse the present-day obsession with the compulsive confessions and splurging of confidences Sennett worried about thirty years ago. The purpose of making sounds and tapping messages is no longer to submit the innards of the soul to the partner's inspection and approval. The words voiced or typed no longer struggle to report the voyage of spiritual discovery. As Chris Moss admirably put it (in *Guardian Weekend*),[11] in and through 'our internet chatting, mobile phoning, 24-hour texting' 'introspection is replaced by a frantic, frivolous interaction that exposes our deepest secrets alongside our shopping list.' Let me comment though that the 'interaction', in spite of being frantic, may not seem that frivolous after all once you realize and remember that the point – its sole point – is to keep the chat going. Providers of internet access are not priests sanctifying the inviolability of unions. The unions have nothing to lean on but our chatting and texting; the union only goes so far as the dialling, talking, messaging. Stop talking – and you are out. Silence equals exclusion. *Il n'y a pas dehors du texte*, indeed – there is nothing outside the text – though not just in the sense meant by Derrida . . .

OM, the glossy magazine attached to one of the most venerable, respected and loved Sunday papers, addressed to, and avidly read and discussed by, the likes of the jet-sets or Bloomsbury or Chelsea sets and all the rest, or almost, of the chattering classes . . .

Take, at random, the issue of 16 June 2002 – though in this case the date does not matter much, because the contents, with minor variations, are immune to the convulsions, leaps or turnabouts of grand history-in-the-making, and to all politics except life politics. The accelerations or slow downs of grand-politics time pass them by . . .

About half of the *OM* magazine, week in week out, is filled by a section called 'Life'. Editors explain: 'Life' is 'the manual for modern living'. The section has its subsections: first comes 'fashion' which informs on the trials and tribulations of 'putting on make-up', with a sub-subsection 'her fashion', which exhorts readers to 'go the extra distance to find the right pair' of shoes. It is followed by the subsection 'Interiors' with a brief interlude on 'doll houses'. Then comes the 'Gardens' part, advising how to 'keep up appearances' and 'impress the guests', in spite of the irksome truth that 'a gardener's work is never done.' The next is the 'Food' subsection, closely followed by the 'Restaurants' part, which advises where to look for tasty food when dining out, and the 'Wine' part, suggesting where to find tasty wine to be consumed when at home. Having reached this point, the reader is well prepared to peruse the three pages of the subsection on 'Living' – unpacked as 'love, sex, family, friends'.

This week, 'Living' is devoted to SDCs – 'semi-detached couples', 'relationship revolutionaries', who 'have burst the suffocating "couple bubble"' and 'go their own ways'. Their twosomeness is part-time. They abhor the idea of sharing home and household, preferring to keep their separate abodes, bank accounts and circles of friends, and share time and space when they feel like it – but not when they don't. Like the old-style work that has split nowadays into a succession of flexible times, odd jobs or short-term projects, and like the old-style property purchase or lease that tends to be replaced these days with time-share occupation and package holidays – the old-style 'till death us do part' marriage, already elbowed out by the self-admittedly temporary 'we will see how it works' cohabitation, is replaced by a part-time, flexible-times 'comings together'.

Experts, as the well-known habit of experts would lead readers to expect, are divided. Their opinions range from a welcoming of the SDC model as the long-sought nirvana (squaring the circle of genuine giving and taking unpaid for by the loss of independence) finally come true, all the way to the condemnation of SDC practitioners for their cowardice: their unwillingness to face up to the tests and hardships that the creation and perpetuation of fully fledged relationship necessarily entail. Pros and cons are painstakingly traced, solemnly pondered and scrupulously weighed, though the effect of the SDC lifestyle on the SDC's human environment (curiously, considering the ecological sensitivity of our age) appears on none of the balance sheets.

After 'Living' has made its point, what is needed to fill the remainder of 'Life'? There are subsections called 'Health', 'Well-being', 'Nutrition' (note: separate from 'Food', 'Restaurants' and 'Wine') and 'Style' (fully made up of furniture commercials). The section is completed with the 'Horoscope' part – in which, depending on their birth dates, some readers are advised to 'forget plodding – mobility is essential now. You have to scoot about, jabber into your mobile and do deals', while others are told that 'it's just your kind of time – new beginnings all round and not too much old business to weigh down your ever optimistic soul.'

In and Out of the Toolbox
of Sociality

Homo sexualis: orphaned and bereaved

As Claude Lévi-Strauss argued, the meeting of the sexes is the
ground on which nature and culture first met; it is by the same
token the starting point, the origin of all culture. Sex was the first
ingredient of the natural endowment of *homo sapiens* on which
artificial, conventional, arbitrary distinctions – the staple industry
of all culture (most prominently, the first act of culture, prohib-
ition of incest: division of females into categories eligible and non-
eligible for sexual cohabitation) – were carved.

It is easy to see that this role of sex was not accidental. Of many
'natural' drives, inclinations and propensities of humans, sexual
desire was and remains the most obviously, unambiguously, un-
assailably *social*. It stretches towards another human being; it calls
for the presence of another human being, and strives to reforge
that presence into a union. It yearns for togetherness; it renders
any human being, however accomplished and in other respects
self-sufficient, incomplete and wanting – unless united with another.

From the encounter of the sexes culture was born. In that
encounter culture first practised its creative art of differentiation.
Never since has the intimate cooperation of culture and nature
in everything sexual been suspended, let alone abandoned. *Ars*

38

erotica, the eminently cultural creation, was from then on to guide the sexual drive towards its fulfilment in human togetherness.

A few isolated exceptions apart, says the leading German sexologist Volkmar Sigusch, our culture 'has brought forth no *ars erotica* but a *scientia sexualis* instead'.[1]

It looks as if Anteros, Eros's brother and the 'vengeful genius of rejected love', has taken over from his dethroned brother the rule over the kingdom of sex. 'Today, sexuality no longer epitomizes the potential for pleasure and happiness. It is no longer mystified, positively, as ecstasy and transgression, but negatively instead, as the source of oppression, inequality, violence, abuse, and deadly infection.'

Anteros was reputedly a highly passionate, prurient, excitable and hot-tempered fellow, but once he became the undisputed lord of the realm he must have forbidden passions among his subjects and proclaimed sex to be a rational, soberly calculated, all-risks-counted, rule-following, and above all totally demystified and disenchanted action. 'The gaze of scientists', says Sigusch, 'was always cool and detached: there were to be no secrets.' Result? 'Today everyone is in the know, and no one has the faintest idea.'

Not that such a frustrating effect of cool posture and detached view detracted from the authority of Anteros, and of his agency, *scientia sexualis* – nor tapered the ranks of their devoted, grateful and expectant followers. Demand for services (for new and improved services, yet 'more of the same' nevertheless) tends to grow, not diminish, as the services repeatedly fail to deliver on their promise. 'Sexual science continues to exist nevertheless, because sexual misery has refused to disappear.'

Scientia sexualis promised to deliver *homini sexuali* from their misery; it goes on promising to do just that, and its promises continue to be trusted and believed for the simple reason that once cut off from all other human modalities and left solely to their own devices, *homini sexuali* have become 'natural objects' for scientific scrutiny – at home only in the laboratory and the therapist's surgery, and visible to themselves and others solely in the light of scientist-operated projectors. Besides, the orphaned and bereaved *homo sexualis* has nowhere else to turn for advice, succour and help.

Orphaned by Eros. Eros, to be sure, is not dead. But exiled from his hereditary realm he has been – as once was Ahaspher, the Wandering Jew – sentenced to loiter and gad about, to roam the streets in a never-ending, since forever vain, search of shelter. Eros is now to be found everywhere, but nowhere will he stay for long. He has no permanent address – if you wish to catch him, write to *poste restante* and keep hoping.

Bereaved by the future. And so by the anticipation and commitment that are the future's legitimate and monopolistic property. Abandoned by the spectre of fatherhood or motherhood, those messengers of eternity and the Great Beyond which used to hover above sexual encounters and rub off on the bodily union some of their surreal mystique and of that sublime blend of faith and apprehension, of joy and dread, which was their trademark.

Medicine competes with sex these days for the charge over 'reproduction'.
Medicine men compete with *homini sexuali* for the role of the principal *auctores* of the drama. The outcome of the competition is a foregone conclusion: thanks to what medicine can do; but also thanks to what medicine is expected to do and what is desired from it, by the pupils and alumni of the market school of consumer life. The bewitching prospect just round the corner is the chance (to quote Sigusch again) to 'choose a child from a catalogue of attractive donors in much the same way as they [contemporary consumers] are accustomed to ordering from mail-order houses or through fashion journals' – and to acquire that child of one's own choice at the time of one's own choice. It would be contrary to the nature of a seasoned consumer not to wish to turn that corner.

40

There were times (of households/workshops, of family farms) when children were *producers*.

In those times, the division of labour and the distribution of family roles overlapped. The child was to join the family *oikos*, to add to the labour force of the workshop or farm – and so in those times when wealth was derived or squeezed from labour, the arrival of a child was expected to improve the well-being of the family. Children could be treated harshly and kept on a short string, but so were all other labourers. Work was not expected to bring joy and serve the employee's pleasure – the idea of 'job satisfaction' was not yet invented. And yet children were, in everybody's view, good investments, and welcomed as such. The more of them the better. Moreover, the advice of reason was to hedge your bets, since life expectation was short and it was everybody's guess whether the newborn would live long enough for its contribution to the family income to be felt. For the authors of the Bible, God's promise to Abraham – 'I will multiply thy seed as the stars of the heaven, and as the sand which is upon the sea shore' – was, unequivocally, a blessing – though many of our contemporaries would rather sense in it a menace, a curse, or both.

There were times (of family fortunes passed from generation to generation down the family tree, and of hereditary social standing) when children were bridges between mortality and immortality, between the abominably short individual life and a (hopefully) infinite duration of the kin. To die childless meant never to build such a bridge. The death of a childless man (though not necessarily of a childless woman, unless she was a queen or suchlike) meant the death of the kin – the most important of duties neglected, the most imperative of tasks unfulfilled.

With the new frailty of family structures, with many a family's life expectation shorter than the individual life expectation of any of its members, with the membership of a particular family lineage turning fast into one of the 'undecidables' of the liquid modern era, and the allegiance to any one of the several available kinship networks turning for a rising number of individuals into a matter of choice, and a *revocable*, until-further-notice choice – a child may be still 'a bridge' to something more durable. But the shore to which that bridge leads is covered in fog that no one expects to disperse, and so it is unlikely to arouse much emotion, let alone feed an action-inspiring desire. Were a sudden gust of wind to blow the fog away, no one knows for sure what kind of shore would be revealed and whether any land firm enough to sustain a permanent home would emerge from the mist. Bridges leading to nowhere, or to nowhere in particular: Who needs them? What for? Who would spend time and good money to design and build them?

Ours are times when the child is, first and foremost, an object of emotional consumption.

Objects of consumption serve the needs, desires or wishes of the consumer; so do children. Children are wanted for the joys of the parental pleasures it is hoped they will bring – the kinds of joys no other object of consumption, however ingenious and sophisticated, can offer. To the sadness of the practitioners of commerce, the commodity market cannot supply worthy substitutes, though the sorrow finds some compensation in the ever-expanding place the world of commerce gains in the production and maintenance of the real thing.

When it comes to objects of consumption, the expected satisfaction tends to be measured against the cost; one looks for 'value for money'.

Children are among the most expensive purchases that average consumers are likely to make in the course of their entire lives. In purely monetary terms, children cost more than a luxurious state-of-the-art car, a round-the-world cruise, even a mansion to be proud of. Worse still, the total cost is likely to grow over the years and its volume cannot be fixed in advance nor estimated with any degree of certainty. In a world that no longer offers reliable career tracks and stable jobs, for people moving from one project to another and earning their living as they move, signing a mortgage contract with undisclosed and indefinitely long repayments means exposure to an uncharacteristically high level of risk and a prolific source of anxiety and fear. One is likely to think twice before signing, and the more one thinks the more the risks involved become obvious, and no amount of deliberation and soul-searching will remove the tinge of doubt that is bound to adulterate the joy. Besides, having children is in our times a matter of decision, not an accident – a circumstance that adds further to the anxiety. Having children or not having them is arguably the most consequential and far-reaching decision there is, and so it is also the most nerve-straining and tension-generating decision one is likely to confront in the course of an entire life.

Moreover, not all the costs are monetary, and those that are not cannot be measured and calculated at all. They defy the trained capacities and propensities of the kind of rational agents we are all trained and struggling to be. 'Creating a family' is like jumping headlong into uncharted waters of unfathomed depth. Forfeiting or postponing other seductive consumer joys of an attraction as yet untried, unknown and impossible to predict, itself an awesome sacrifice stridently jarring with the habits of a prudent consumer, is not its only likely consequence.

Having children means weighing the welfare of another, weaker and dependent, being against one's own comfort. The autonomy of one's own preferences is bound to be compromised, and ever anew: year by year; daily. One may become, horror of horrors, 'dependent'. Having children may mean the need to lower one's professional ambitions, to 'sacrifice a career', as the people sitting in judgement over professional performance would look askance at any sign of divided loyalty. Most painfully, having children means accepting such loyalty-dividing dependence for an indefinite time, entering an open-ended and irrevocable commitment with no 'until further notice' clause attached; the kind of obligation that goes against the grain of liquid modern life politics and which most people at most times zealously avoid in the other manifestations of their lives. Awakening to such a commitment may be a traumatic experience. Post-natal depression and post-childbirth marital (or partnership) crises look like specifically 'liquid modern' ailments, in the same way as anorexia, bulimia, and countless varieties of allergy.

The joys of parenthood come, as it were, in a package deal with the sorrows of self-sacrifice and the fears of unexplored dangers.

A sober, reliable calculation of gains and losses stays stubbornly and vexingly beyond the would-be-parents' reach and comprehension.

Risks are involved in any consumer acquisition – but the traders of other consumer goods, and particularly of goods misnamed as 'durable', fall over backwards to assure the prospective clients that the risks they are taking have been reduced to a minimum. They offer guarantees, extended guarantees (even if only a few of them can vouch in good conscience that the company issuing the guarantee will survive until the guarantee runs out, and virtually none can assure the clients that the attractions of the purchased commodity that keep it away from the rubbish bin will not fade well before that), money-back guarantees, and promises of a long or lifelong aftersales service. Credible or untrustworthy as such guarantees might be, none is available in the case of child-birth.

No wonder that medical research institutes and pregnancy clinics are awash with commercial companies' money. There is potentially an infinite demand for reducing the risks endemic in childbirth at least to the level claimed on behalf of the commodities on the store-shelf. Companies offering the chance to 'choose a child from a catalogue of attractive donors' and bespoke clinics composing the gene spectrum of an unborn child to the client's order need not worry about a lack of interested clients, or a shortage of profitable business.

To sum up: the widely noted separation of sex from reproduction is power-assisted. It is a joint product of the liquid modern life setting, and of consumerism as the chosen and sole available strategy of 'seeking biographical solutions to socially produced problems' (Ulrich Beck). It is the mixture of those two factors that leads to a shifting of reproduction and childbirth issues away from sex and into an entirely different sphere, operated by a totally different logic and set of rules than sexual activity. The bereavement of *homo sexualis* is overdetermined.

As if in anticipation of the pattern that was to prevail in our times, Erich Fromm attempted to explain the attraction of 'sex as such' (sex 'in its own right', sex practised separately from its orthodox functions), referring to its quality as a (misleading) answer to the all-too-human 'craving for complete fusion' through an 'illusion of union'.[2]

Union – because this is exactly what men and women keenly seek when desperate to escape the loneliness they already suffer or fear is to come. Illusion – because the union reached in the brief moment of orgasmic climax 'leaves strangers as far apart as they were before' so that 'they feel their estrangement even more markedly than before'. In that role, sexual orgasm 'assumes a function which makes it not very different from alcoholism and drug addiction'. Like them, it is intense – but 'transitory and periodical'.[3]

The union is illusionary and the experience is bound to be frustrating in the end, says Fromm, because of the separation of the union from love (that is, let me explain, from the *fürsein* kind of relationship; from an intentionally lasting, indefinite commitment to the partner's well-being). In Fromm's view, sex may only be an instrument of *genuine* fusion – instead of being an ephemeral, duplicitous and ultimately self-destructive *impression* of a fusion – thanks to its conjunction with love. Whatever union-generating capacity sex may possess rubs off from its companionship with love.

Since Fromm wrote, the isolation of sex from other realms of life has progressed further than ever before.

Today, sex is the very epitome, perhaps the silent/secret archetype, of that 'pure relationship' (an oxymoron, to be sure: human relationships tend to fill, infest and modify all nooks and crannies, however remote, of the *Lebenswelt* and so can be anything but 'pure') which, as Anthony Giddens suggests, has become the prevailing target/ideal model of human partnership. Sex is now expected to be self-sustained and self-sufficient, to 'stand on its own feet', to be judged solely by the satisfaction it may bring on its own (even if it stops as a rule well short of the expectations beefed up by the media). No wonder that its capacity to spawn frustration, and to exacerbate the very same sensation of estrangement it was hoped to heal, has also grown enormously. Sex's victory in the great war of independence has been, in the best of circumstances, pyrrhic. The wonder drug appears to produce ailments and sufferings no less numerous and arguably more acute than those it promised to cure.

Orphaning and bereavement were for a brief time celebrated as the ultimate liberation of sex from the prison in which patriarchal, puritan, still-haplessly-Victorian, spoilsport, killjoy and hypocritical society held it.
Here, at long last, there was a purer than pure relationship, an encounter that served no other purpose but pleasure and joy. A dream happiness without strings attached, a happiness unafraid of side-effects and so cheerfully oblivious to its consequences, a happiness of the 'if not fully satisfied, return product for full refund' kind: a fullest incarnation of freedom, as the popular wisdom and practice of consumer society has defined it.

It is all right, perhaps even exhilarating and altogether wonderful, for sex to be so liberated. The snag is how to hold it in place once the ballast has been thrown overboard; how to hold it in shape if frames are no longer available. Flying lightly is mirth, rudderless flying is distress. Change is blissful, volatility annoying. The unbearable lightness of sex?

Volkmar Sigusch is a practising therapist; daily, he meets the casualties of 'pure sex'. He records their complaints – and the list of grievances calling for the expert's intervention lengthens unstoppably. His summaries of findings are as sombre as they are sober.

> All forms of intimate relationships currently in vogue bear the same mask of false happiness once worn by marital and later by free love...[A]s we took a closer look and pulled away the mask, we found unfulfilled yearnings, ragged nerves, disappointed love, hurts, fears, loneliness, hypocrisy, egotism, and repetition compulsion...Performances have replaced ecstasy, physics are in, metaphysics out... Abstinence, monogamy, and promiscuity are all equally far removed from the free life of sensuality that none of us knows.[4]

Technical concerns square ill with emotions. Concentration on performance leaves no time or room for ecstasy. Physics is not the road to metaphysics. It was emotion, ecstasy and metaphysics from which the seductive power of sex used to flow – as it would do now, but the mystery is gone and so the yearnings cannot but stay unfulfilled...

When sex stands for a physiological event in the body and 'sensuality' invokes little except a pleasurable bodily sensation, sex is not liberated from supernumerary, superfluous, useless, cumbersome and cramping loads. It is, on the contrary, *overloaded*. Overflowing with expectations beyond its capacity to deliver.

Intimate connections of sex with love, security, permanence, immortality-through-continuation-of-kin were not after all as useless and constraining as they were thought and felt and charged to be. The old and allegedly old-fashioned companions of sex were perhaps its necessary supports (necessary not for the technical perfection of the performance, but for its gratifying potential). Perhaps the contradictions with which sexuality is endemically fraught are no more likely to be resolved (mitigated, defused, neutralized) in the absence of 'strings attached', than they could be in their presence. Perhaps those strings were feats of cultural ingenuity rather than tokens of cultural misconception or failure.

Liquid modern rationality recommends light cloaks and condemns steel casings.

In lasting commitments, liquid modern reason spies out oppression; in durable engagement, it sees incapacitating dependency. That reason denies rights to bindings and bonds, spatial or temporal. There is neither need nor use for them that the liquid modern rationality of consumers could justify. Bindings and bonds make human relations 'impure' – as they would do to any act of consumption that assumes instant satisfaction and similarly instant obsolescence of the consumed object. Defence attorneys of 'impure relations' would face an uphill struggle trying to convince the jurors and win their consent.

Sigusch believes that sooner or later 'the wishes and desires that escape the grasp of rationality' will make a comeback – and with a vengeance – and when they do, we won't be able to respond 'without resorting to the use of concepts about natural instincts and eternal values that have been corrupted, historically and politically, to the core'.

Were it to happen, though, as Sigusch augurs or portends, it would call for more than just a new view of sex and of the expectations that may be legitimately invested in sexual acts. It would call for nothing less than the exemption of sex from the sovereignty of consumer rationality. Perhaps it would call for more yet: for consumer rationality to be deprived of, and to shed, its present-day sovereignty over the motives and strategies of human life politics. This would mean, however, calling for more than could be reasonably expected to happen in the foreseeable future.

'The wishes and desires that escape the grasp of rationality' (liquid modern, consumer rationality to be exact) were inseparably and seamlessly tied to sex since sex, like other human activities, was woven into the model of a producer's life.

Within that model neither love 'till death us do part', nor building bridges to eternity, nor consent to 'giving hostages to fate' and to no-going-back commitments were redundant – let alone perceived as confining or oppressive. On the contrary, they used to be the 'natural instincts' of the *homo faber*, just as they go now against the equally 'natural' instincts of the *homo consumens*. Nor were they, by any account, 'irrational'. On the contrary, they were the must-be and should-be accoutrements or manifestations of *homo faber*'s rationality. Love and willingness to procreate were indispensable companions to *homo faber*'s sex, just as the lasting unions they helped to create were 'main products' – not 'side-effects', let alone the rejects or wastage, of sexual acts.

To each gain, its losses. To each achievement, its price.

Whatever the horror and revulsion with which the losses suffered and the prices paid in the past are remembered or recalled, it is the losses borne today and the prices to be paid tomorrow that annoy and grieve most. No point in measuring past and present

48

distresses against each other, trying to find out which of the two is less bearable. Each anguish hurts and torments in its own time.

Today's agonies of *homo sexualis* are those of *homo consumens*. They have been born together. If they ever go away, they will march shoulder to shoulder.

Sexual capacity was *homo faber*'s building tool used in the construction and maintenance of human relations.

When deployed on the building site of human bonds, sexual need/desire prodded *homo sexualis* to stay on the job and see it through once started. The builders wished the outcome of their efforts, like one wishes all buildings, to be solidly constructed, durable and (ideally forever) reliable.

All too often the builders had too much confidence in their designing powers to worry about the feelings of the intended resident(s). Respect is, after all, but one edge of a two-edged sword of care, whose other edge is oppression. Indifference and contempt are two reefs on which many an earnest ethical intention has foundered, and moral selves need a lot of vigilance and navigation skills to sail safe between them. This said, it seems nevertheless that morality – that *Fürsein* dictated by the responsibility for anOther and put in operation once it has been taken up – was, with all its breathtaking vistas and all its sidetracks, ambushes and treacherous deviations, made to the measure of *homo faber*.

Freed from building tasks and resentful of building efforts, *homo consumens* may deploy sexual powers in novel, imaginative ways. *Fürsein*, though, is not one of them.

Consumerism is not about *accumulating* goods (who gathers goods must put up as well with heavy suitcases and cluttered houses), but about *using* them and *disposing* of them after use to make room for other goods and their uses.

Consumer life favours lightness and speed; also the novelty and variety that lightness and speed are hoped to foster and expedite. It is the turnover, not the volume of purchases, that measures success in the life of *homo consumens*.

49

The usability of the goods as a rule outlives their usefulness to the consumer. But if used repeatedly, the purchased commodity thwarts the search for variety, and with each successive use the veneer of novelty rubs away and wipes off. Woe to those who, because of a dearth of assets, are doomed to go on using goods that no longer hold a promise of new and untried sensations; woe to those who for the same reason are stuck with one good instead of browsing through the full, and apparently inexhaustible, assortment. Such people are the outcasts in the society of consumers, the flawed consumers, the inadequates and the incompetents, the flops; the emaciated starvelings amidst the opulence of the consumer feast.

Those who need not hold on to their utilities for long, and certainly not long enough to let tedium set in, come out on top. In the society of consumers, prestidigitator is the figure of success. Were it not anathema to the purveyors of consumer goods, consumers true to their fate and character would develop the habit of hiring things rather than purchasing them. Unlike the sellers of commodities, hiring companies, temptingly, promise to regularly replace hired goods with the latest state-of-the-art models. The sellers, not to be outdone, promise to return money if the client 'is not fully satisfied' and if (hoping that the satisfaction won't evaporate that quickly) the bought goods are returned within, say, ten days.

'Purification' of sex allows sexual practice to be adapted to such advanced shopping/hiring patterns. 'Pure sex' is construed with some form of reliable money-back guarantee in view – and the partners in a 'purely sexual encounter' may feel secure, aware that 'no strings attached' compensates for the vexing frailty of their engagement.

Thanks to a clever advertising stratagem, the vernacular meaning of 'safe sex' has recently been reduced to the use of condoms. The slogan would not be such a commercial success if it did not strike a raw nerve in millions who desire their sexual exploits to be insured against undesirable (since uncontrollable) consequences. It is after all the general strategy of a promotion to present the product on offer as the sought-after solution to the worries that either have been already haunting its prospective buyers or have been freshly contrived to suit its advertised potential.

More often than not, the advertising copy substitutes a part for the whole; sales capitalize on supplies of anguish far in excess of the advertised product's healing capacity. Indeed, using a condom protects sexual partners against HIV infection. But such an infection is but one of a great number of unanticipated and certainly unbargained-for consequences of sexual encounters that make *homo sexualis* desirous of sex being 'safe'. Let out of a cramped, yet closely managed harbour and having set sail into uncharted waters without a map or compass, sex began to feel decidedly 'unsafe' well before the discovery of AIDS supplied the focal point and the label for diffuse and unnamed fears.

The most fearsome of fears stemmed from the ambiguity of the sexual encounter: was it an initial step towards a relationship, or its crowning and its terminus? A stage in a meaningful succession or a one-off episode, a means to an end or a self-contained act? No union of bodies, however hard one might try, can escape social framing and cut out all connections with other facets of social existence. Sex stripped of its former social standing and socially endorsed meanings encapsulated the harrowing and alarming uncertainty that was to become the major bane of liquid modern living.

The entitlements of sexual partners have become the prime site of anxiety. What sort of commitment, if any, does the union of bodies entail? In what way, if any, does it bind the future of the partners? Can the sexual encounter be kept in isolation from the rest of life's pursuits, or will it (will it tend to, will it be allowed to) spill over across that rest of life, saturate it and transform it?

In itself, sexual union is short-lived; in the partners' life, it is an *episode*. As Milan Kundera points out, an episode 'is not an unavoidable consequence of preceding action, nor the cause of what is to follow'.[5] That immaculate conception cum sterility, the essential non-infectiousness, is an episode's beauty – and so, we may say, it is also the beauty of a sexual encounter as long as it remains an episode. The snag, however, is that 'nobody can guarantee that some totally episodic event may not contain within itself a power that some day could unexpectedly turn into a cause of further events.' To cut a long story short: 'no episode is *a priori* condemned to remain an episode for ever.' No episode is safe from its consequences. The ensuing unsafety is eternal. Uncertainty will never fully and irrevocably dissipate. It may only be suspended for a time of unknown duration – but the hold of the suspension is itself shot with doubts and so becomes another source of irksome insecurity.

Marriage, one may say, is the acceptance of the consequentiality which casual encounters refuse to accept (at least a declaration of intent to accept it – for the duration of the wedlock).

In such a case, ambiguity is resolved, and uncertainty is replaced by a certainty that acts do matter beyond their own timespan and carry consequences that may last longer than their causes. Uncertainty is exiled from the lives of the partners and its return is barred for as long as the termination of the marriage is not contemplated.

But can uncertainty be banished without acceding to such a condition, a price which many partners would find too heavy to pay? If one can never be sure, as Kundera suggests, that the episode was indeed but an episode, this cannot be done. But one can still try, and one does try, and however adverse the odds one can hardly stop trying to turn them in one's own favour.

Reputedly, Parisians try harder than many, and with more ingenuity. In Paris, *échangisme* (a new and, given the new equality of sexes, more politically correct name for the somewhat older concept, redolent of patriarchalism, of wife-swapping) has allegedly become the vogue, the most popular game and the main talk of the town.

Les échangistes kill two birds with one stone. First, they loosen a little of the grip of marital commitment, having agreed to make its consequences somewhat less consequential and therefore the uncertainty generated by the endemic unclarity of prospects somewhat less harrowing. Second, they acquire trustworthy accomplices in their effort to fend off the loitering, and therefore potentially irritating, consequences of the sexual encounter – since all interested sides, having been participants in the event and thus wishing to prevent it from spilling out of the episode's frame, are sure to join in the fending off.

As a strategy to fight off the spectre of uncertainty with which sexual episodes are known to be pregnant, *échangisme* has a distinct advantage over 'one-night stands' and similarly chancy and short-lived encounters. Protection against undesirable consequences is here another person's duty and worry, and in the worst of circumstances it is not a solitary endeavour but a task shared with mighty and dedicated allies. The advantage of *échangisme* over mere 'extramarital adultery' is particularly blatant. None of the *échangistes* is betrayed, no one's interests are threatened, and as in Habermas's ideal model of 'undistorted communication' everyone is a participant. *Ménage à quatre* (or *six, huit,* etc. – the more the better) is free of all the blights and deficiencies known to be the bane of the *ménage à trois*.

As one would expect when the purpose and the stake of the enterprise is to chase away the phantom of insecurity, *échangisme* seeks entrenchment in contractual institutions and the support of the law. One becomes an *échangiste* by joining a club, signing a form, promising to obey the rules (and hoping that all the others around have done the same) and being issued with a membership card to ensure entry and to make sure that whoever is in is simultaneously a player and a game. Since everyone likely to be met inside is aware of the purpose of the club and its rules and has promised to observe both, all argument or use of force, all consent-seeking, hazards of seduction and other awkward and precarious preliminaries plagued with uncertain results have been made redundant.

Or so it seems, for a time. The *échangisme* conventions may, as credit cards once promised, take the waiting out of wanting. Like most recent technological innovations, they shorten the distance between the want and its satisfaction and make the passage from the one to the other faster and less burdened with effort. They may also prevent a partner from claiming more benefits than the episodic encounter allows.

Would they, however, defend *homo sexualis* against himself (or herself)? Would the unfulfilled yearnings, love's frustrations, fears

53

of loneliness and of being hurt, hypocrisy and guilt be left behind after a visit to the club? Would closeness, joy, tenderness, affection and pride be found there? Well, the visitor may say with good conscience: this is sex, stupid – it has nothing to do with this, that, or anything else for that matter. But if she or he is right, does sex itself matter? Or rather, to repeat after Sigusch, if the substance of sexual activity is the derivation of instant pleasure, 'then it is no longer important what is done but simply *that* it happens.'

Commenting on the highly influential *Bodies that Matter: On the Discursive Limits of Sex* by Judith Butler,[6] Sigusch points out that 'according to the female theorists now setting the tone in the gender discourse, both sex and gender are determined entirely by culture, devoid of all natural nature and thus alterable, transitory, and capable of being subverted.'

It seems though that the nature–culture opposition is not the best frame in which to inscribe the dilemmas of the current sex/gender quandary. The true point of contention is the extent to which various types of sexual proclivities/preferences/identities are flexible, alterable, and dependent on the subject's choice; but the oppositions between culture and nature, and between 'it is a matter of choice' and 'humans cannot help it and can do nothing about it', no longer overlap in the way they did through a better part of modern history and until recently. In popular discourse, culture increasingly stands for the inherited part of identity that neither could nor should be tinkered with (unless at the tinkerer's peril), whereas the traits and the attributes traditionally classified as 'natural' (hereditary, gene-transmitted) are ever more often presented as amenable to human manipulation and so open to choice – a choice for which, as in all choice, the chooser should feel responsible and be seen by others to be so.

It does not therefore matter so much whether sexual predilections (articulated as 'sexual identity') are 'endowments of nature' or 'cultural constructs'. What does matter is whether it is up to *homo sexualis* to determine (discover or invent) which one (or more) of the multitude of sexual identities fits her or him best, or whether, like *homo sapiens* in the case of the 'community of birth', she or he is bound to embrace that fate and live their life in a manner that recasts unalterable fate into personal vocation.

Whatever vocabulary is used to articulate the current plight of *homo sexualis*, and whether self-training and self-discovery or genetic and medical interventions are viewed as the right way to the proper/desirable sexual identity, the bottom line still remains the 'alterability', transience, non-finality of any of the assumed sexual identities. The life of *homo sexualis* is for that reason fraught with anxiety. There is always a suspicion – even if it is put to sleep and dormant for a time – that one is living a lie or a mistake; that something crucially important has been overlooked, missed, neglected, left untried and unexplored; that a vital obligation to one's own authentic self has not been met, or that some chances of unknown happiness completely different from any happiness experienced before have not been taken up in time and are bound to be lost forever if they continue to be neglected.

Homo sexualis is doomed to remain permanently incomplete and unfulfilled – even at an age when the sexual fire would in the past have quickly died down but is now expected to be fanned back into flame by the joint efforts of miraculous fitness regimes and wonder drugs. This journey never ends, the itinerary is recomposed at each station, and the final destination remains unknown throughout.

The underdefinition, incompleteness and non-finality of sexual identity (just like all the other facets of identity in liquid modern surroundings) are a poison and its antidote blended into one powerful anti-tranquilizer superdrug.

Awareness of this ambivalence is unnerving and breeds no end of anxiety; it gestates uncertainty that can be only temporarily cooled, never fully extinguished. It contaminates any chosen/attained condition with gnawing doubts as to its propriety and wisdom. But it also protects against the humiliation of under-achievement or failure. There is always the possibility of blaming a mistaken choice, rather than an inability to live up to the opportunities it offered, for the failure of the anticipated bliss to materialize. There is always a chance to abandon the road along which

55

fulfilment was sought and to start again – even, if the prospects look attractive, from scratch.

The combined effect of the poison and the antidote is to keep *homo sexualis* perpetually on the move, pushed ('this type of sexuality failed to bring the peak experience I was told to expect') and pulled ('other types I saw and heard of are within reach – it's just a matter of resolve and trying hard').

Homo sexualis is not a state, let alone a permanent, immutable state, but a process, laden with trials and errors, hazardous voyages of discovery and occasional finds, interspersed with numerous slips, sorrows of missed chances and joys of looming relishes.

In his essay on 'civilized' sexual morality[7] Sigmund Freud suggests that civilization rests in great measure on the exploitation and deployment of the natural human capacity to 'sublimate' sexual instincts: 'to exchange [the] originally sexual aim for another one' – particularly socially useful causes.

To achieve that effect, the 'natural' outlets of sexual instincts (both auto-erotic and object-erotic) are repressed – cut altogether or at least partly blocked. The untapped and unused sexual drive is then redirected through socially constructed conduits to socially constructed targets. 'The forces that can be employed for cultural activities are thus to a great extent obtained through the suppression of what are known as the *perverse* elements of sexual excitation.'

After Derrida, we may be excused for suspecting a fatal circularity in the last proposition. Certain 'elements of sexual excitation' 'are known as perverse' because they resist suppression and therefore cannot be employed for what have been defined as cultural (that is, worthy) activities. More to the point, however, for *homo sexualis* inserted in the liquid modern setting the boundary separating the 'healthy' and the 'perverse' manifestations of sexual instincts is all but blurred. All forms of sexual activity are not just tolerated, but often suggested as useful therapy for one or another psychological ailment, increasingly accepted as legitimate routes in the individual pursuit of happiness, and encouraged to be displayed in public. (Paedophilia and child pornography are possibly the sole outlets of sexual drive still almost unanimously decried as perverse. On that point, though, Sigusch comments, caustically yet correctly, that the secret of such uncharacteristic unanimity may lie in the fact that the opposition to child pornography 'requires us to expend nothing but the oil of humanism that has so effectively lubricated the wheels of violence before. Only a few, however, are seriously in favour of programmes capable of saving children's lives, as that would cost money and comfort while requiring the adoption of a different way of living.')

In our liquid modern times the powers-that-be no longer seem interested in drawing the boundary between 'right' and 'perverse' sex. The reason perhaps is the fast fading demand for the employment of spare sexual energy in the service of 'civilizing causes' (read: production of discipline over the patterns of routine behaviour functional in a society of producers) – a departure which Freud, writing at the start of the past century, could hardly guess, let alone visualize.

The 'socially useful' objects offered for sexual discharge need no longer be disguised as 'cultural causes'; they parade, with pride and above all with great profit, their endemic or contrived sexuality. After the era in which sexual energy had to be sublimated in order to keep the car assembly line moving came an era when sexual energy needed to be beefed up, given freedom to select any channel of discharge at hand and encouraged to go rampant, so that cars leaving the assembly line might be lusted after as sexual objects.

It seems that the link between the sublimation of sexual instinct and its repression, deemed by Freud to be an indispensable condition of any orderly social arrangement, has been broken. Liquid modern society has found a way of exploiting the human propensity/amenability to sublimate sexual instincts without resorting to their repression at all, or at least radically limiting its extent. That happened thanks to the progressive deregulation of the sublimating processes, now diffuse and dispersed, perpetually changing direction and guided by seduction by the objects of sexual desire on offer rather than by any coercive pressures.

Communitas for sale

When the quality lets you down, you seek salvation in quantity. When duration is not on, it is the rapidity of change that may redeem you.

If you feel ill at ease in that fluid world and are lost among the profusion of contradictory road signs that seem to move as if on castors, visit one or some of those expert counsellors for whose services there has never been a greater demand and of whom there has never been a richer supply.

Soothsayers and astrologers of past ages used to tell their clients what their predecided, unswerving and implacable fate would be regardless of what they might do or refrain from doing; the experts of our fluid modern era would most certainly pass the buck back to their confused and perplexed clients.

Their clients would find their anxiety traced back to their doings and undoings, and errors would be sought (and surely found) in their ways: not enough self-assertion, not enough self-care or self-drilling, but most probably insufficient flexibility, too tight an embrace of old routines, places or people, a lack of enthusiasm for change and an unwillingness to change once change had to come. The counsellors would advise more self-appreciation, self-concern and self-care, more attention to their clients' inner ability for pleasure and satisfaction – as well as less 'dependence' on others and less attention to others' demands for attention and care; more distance and more sobriety in calculating the balance of reasonable hopes of gains and realistic prospects of losses. Clients who diligently learned the lessons and followed the advice faithfully should from now on ask themselves more often the question 'what is in it for me?' and more resolutely demand from partners and everybody else to give them 'more space' – that is, keep themselves at a distance and not expect, foolishly, that commitments once undertaken are bound to be held forever.

Don't let yourself be caught. Avoid embraces that are too tight. Remember, the deeper and denser your attachments, commitments, engagement, the greater your risk. Do not confuse the network – a swirl of roads to glide over – with a net: that treacherous implement that feels from the inside like a cage.

And remember, of course, that keeping all eggs in one basket is the ultimate folly!

Your mobile always rings (or so you hope).

One message flashes on the screen in hot pursuit of another. Your fingers are always busy: you squeeze the keys, calling new numbers to answer the calls or composing messages of your own. You *stay connected* – even though you are constantly on the move, and though the invisible senders and recipients of calls and messages move as well, all following their own trajectories. Mobiles are for people on the move.

You never leave your mobile out of sight. Your jogging gear has a special pocket for your mobile, and you would not go out with that pocket empty just as you would not go running without your training shoes. As a matter of fact, you would go *nowhere* without your mobile ('nowhere' is, indeed, the space without a mobile, with a mobile out of range, or a mobile with a flat battery). And once with your mobile, you are never *out* or *away*. You are always *in* – but never locked up in one place. Cocooned in a web of calls and messages, you are invulnerable. Those around you cannot blackball you, and if they try, nothing that truly matters would change.

It is unimportant which place you are in, who the people are around you and what you are doing in that place filled with those people. The difference between one place and another, one set of people within your sight and corporeal reach and another, has been cancelled and made null and void. You are the sole stable point in the universe of moving objects – and so are (thanks to you, thanks to you!) your extensions: your connections. Connections will stay unscathed despite the fact that those connected by the connections move. Connections are rocks among the quicksands. On them you can count – and since you trust their solidity, you can stop worrying about how muddy and treacherously slushy the ground under your feet is at a time when a call or a message is sent or received.

A call has not been answered? A message has not been returned? No reason to worry either. There are so many other telephone numbers on the list, and seemingly no limit to the number of messages you may, with the help of a few tiny keys, knead into that little thing that fits so neatly into your hand. Come to think of it (were there time left to think, that is), it is utterly unlikely that you'd ever reach the end of your portable directory or type all the messages that could be typed. There are always more connections to be used – and so it does not terribly matter how many of them might have proved frail and breakable. The rate and pace of wear and tear does not matter either. *Each* connection may be short-lived, but their *excess* is indestructible. Amidst the eternity of the imperishable network, you can feel unthreatened by the irreparable fragility of each single, transient connection.

Into that network you can always run for shelter when the crowd that surrounds you becomes too madding for your taste. Thanks to what is made possible as long as your mobile is securely ensconced in your pocket, you stand out of the crowd – and standing out is the membership application, the term of admission to that crowd.

A crowd of stand-outs: a *swarm*, to be more precise. An aggregate of self-propelled individuals who need no commanding officer, figurehead, haranguer, agent-provocateur or stool-pigeon to keep it together. A mobile aggregate in which each mobile unit does the same, but nothing is done jointly. Units march in step without falling in line. The true-to-form crowd expels the units that stand out, or tramples over them – but it is only such units that the swarm tolerates.

Mobile telephones did not create the swarm, though they no doubt help to keep it as it is – as a swarm. The swarm was waiting for the Nokias and the Ericssons and the Motorolas eager to serve it. Were there no swarm, of what use would the mobiles be?

Those who stay apart, mobiles allow to get in touch. Those who get in touch, mobiles permit to stay apart...

Jonathan Rowe remembers:

In the later 1990s, in the midst of the high tech boom, I spent a lot of time in a coffee shop in the theater district in San Francisco... I observed a scene play out there time and time again. Mom is nursing her mocha. The kids are picking at their muffins, feet dangling from their chairs. And there's Dad, pulled back slightly from the table, talking into his cell phone... It was supposed to be a 'communication revolution', and yet here, in the technological epicentre, the members of this family were avoiding one another's eyes.[8]

Two years later, Rowe would probably see four cell phones in operation around that table. Mobiles would not stop mom nursing her mocha, nor the kids munching their muffins. But they would make avoiding each other's eyes an unnecessary effort: eyes would by then have turned into blank walls anyway – and no harm is done to a blank wall by facing another blank wall. Given enough time, the mobiles would train the eyes to look without seeing.

As John Urry points out, 'the relations of co-presence always involve nearness *and* farness, proximity *and* distance, solidity *and* imagination.'[9] True; but the ubiquitous and continuous presence of the third – of the 'virtual proximity' universally and permanently available thanks to the electronic network – shifts the balance decidedly in favour of farness, distance and imagination. It augurs (or does it portend?) a final separation between 'physically distant' and 'spiritually remote'. The first is no longer a condition of the second. The second now has its own, high-tech 'material basis', infinitely more ample, flexible, variegated, attractive and pregnant with adventure than any rearrangement of material bodies. And physical proximity has less chance than ever of interfering with spiritual farness...

Urry is right in dismissing prophecies of the imminent demise of travel, made redundant by the facility of electronic connection. If anything, the advent of electronically assured out-of-placeness makes travel safer, less risky and off-putting, than ever before – and so it cancels out many of the past limits to the magnetic power of 'going places'. Cell phones signal, materially and symbolically, the ultimate liberation from place. Being near to a socket is no longer a condition of 'staying connected'. Travellers may delete from their calculation of gains and losses the differences between departing and staying, distance and proximity, civilization and wilderness.

Much software and hardware has been dumped on computer graveyards since the unforgettable Peter Sellers tried in vain (in Hal Ashby's film of 1979, *Being There*) to switch off a posse of nuns with the help of a TV remote control. These days he would have no difficulty in deleting them from the picture – the picture *he* saw, *his* picture, the sum total of relevancies in the world within reach. The other side of the *virtual proximity* coin is *virtual distance*: suspension, perhaps even cancellation, of anything that made topographical closeness into proximity. Proximity no longer requires physical closeness; but physical closeness no longer determines proximity.

It is an open question which side of the coin did the most to make the electronic network and its implements of entry and exit such a popular and eagerly used currency of human interaction. Was it the new facility of connecting? Or was it the new facility of cutting the connection? There is no shortage of occasions when the second feels more urgent, and matters more, than the first.

The advent of virtual proximity renders human connections simultaneously more frequent and more shallow, more intense and more brief. Connections tend to be too shallow and brief to condense into bonds. Focused on the business in hand, they are protected against spilling over and engaging the partners beyond the time and the topic of the message dialled and read – unlike what human relationships, notoriously diffuse and voracious, are known to perpetrate. Contacts require less time and effort to be entered and less time and effort to be broken. *Distance is no obstacle to getting in touch – but getting in touch is no obstacle to staying apart.* Spasms of virtual proximity end, ideally, without leftovers and lasting sediments. Virtual proximity can be, both substantively and metaphorically, finished with nothing more than the press of a button.

It seems that the most seminal accomplishment of virtual proximity is the separation between communication and relationship. Unlike the old-style topographical proximity, it neither requires that bonds are established beforehand nor necessarily results in establishing them in consequence. 'Being connected' is less costly than 'being engaged' – but also considerably less productive in terms of bond building and bond maintenance.

Virtual proximity defuses the pressure that non-virtual closeness is in the habit of exerting. It also sets the pattern for all other proximity. All proximity is now bound to measure its merits and shortcomings by the standards of virtual proximity.

Virtual and non-virtual proximity have switched places: it is now the virtual variety of proximity that has become the 'reality' answering Émile Durkheim's classic description: something that fixes, 'institutes outside us, certain ways of acting and certain judgements which do not depend on each particular will taken separately'; something that 'is to be recognized by the power of external coercion' and by the 'resistance offered against every individual act that tends to contravene it'.[10] Non-virtual proximity stops well short of the tough standards of unobtrusiveness and the rigid standards of flexibility that virtual proximity has set. If it fails to imitate what virtual proximity has made into a norm, orthodox topographical proximity will become a 'contravening act' that will surely encounter resistance. And so it is left to virtual proximity to play the role of the genuine, unadulterated, *real* reality by which all other pretenders to the status of reality must measure themselves and be judged.

Everyone has seen, heard, and has not been able to help overhearing fellow passengers on the train speaking non-stop on their telephones. If you were travelling first class, the talkers were mostly businessmen eager to keep busy and look efficient – that is, to connect to as many mobile users as possible and to show that there are indeed many such mobile users ready to take their call. If you were travelling second class, they were mostly teenagers of both sexes and young men and women telling someone at home what station they had just left and what station would be next. You might have had the impression that they were counting the minutes separating them from home and could hardly wait to meet their conversationalists in person. It might not have occurred to you that many of those mobile chats you overheard were not *overtures* to a longer and more substantive conversation at their destination – but a *substitute* for it. That these chats were not preparing the ground for the real stuff, but the real stuff itself... That many of these young people eager to inform invisible listeners of their whereabouts were shortly, upon arrival, to hurry into their separate rooms and lock the doors behind them.

When it was still a few years before the upsurge of electronically operated virtual proximity Michael Schluter and David Lee observed that 'we wear privacy as a pressure suit...Anything but invite encounter; anything but get involved.' Homes are no longer warm islands of intimacy among the fast cooling seas of privacy. Homes have turned from shared playgrounds of love and friendship into the sites of territorial skirmishes, and from building sites of togetherness into the assemblies of fortified bunkers. 'We have stepped into our separate houses and closed the door, and then stepped into our separate rooms and closed the door. The home becomes a multi-purpose leisure centre where household members can live, as it were, separately side by side.'[11]

It would be foolish and irresponsible to blame electronic gadgets for the slow yet consistent recession of personal, direct, face-to-face, multifaceted and multipurpose, continuous proximity. Yet virtual proximity boasts features that in a liquid modern world can be seen, with good reason, as advantageous – but which cannot easily be obtained under conditions of that other, not virtual, *tête-à-tête*. No wonder virtual proximity is given preference and practised with greater zeal and abandon than any other closeness. Loneliness behind the closed door of a private room with a mobile telephone within reach may seem much less risky and safer a condition than sharing the household's common ground.

The more human attention and learning effort is absorbed by the virtual variety of proximity, the less time is dedicated to the acquisition and exercise of skills which the other, non-virtual kind of proximity requires. Such skills fall into disuse – are forgotten, never learned in the first place, are shunned, or are resorted to, if at all, reluctantly. Their deployment, if called for, may present an awkward, perhaps even insurmountable, challenge. This adds further to the allurements of virtual proximity. Once entered, the passage from non-virtual to virtual proximity acquires its own momentum. It looks self-perpetuating; it is also self-accelerating.

'As the generation weaned on the net enters its prime dating years, internet dating is really taking off. And it's not a last resort. It's a recreational activity. It's entertainment.'

So finds Louise France.[12] For today's lonely hearts, discos and singles bars are a distant memory, she concludes. They have not acquired (and do not fear that they have not acquired) enough of the sociability skills that making friends in such places would require. Besides, internet dating has advantages which personal encounters do not have: in the latter, ice once broken may stay broken or melt once and for all – but it is totally different with internet dating. As a twenty-eight-year-old interviewee in a Bath University study confided, 'You can always press delete. It's the easiest thing in the world not to reply to an e-mail.' France comments: users of online dating facilities can date *safely*, secure in the knowledge that they can always return to the marketplace for another bout of shopping. Or, as Dr Jeff Gavin of Bath University, quoted by France, suggests – on the internet one can date 'without fear of "real world" repercussions'. Or this is at any rate how one can feel when shopping for partners on the internet. Just like browsing through the pages of a mail-order catalogue with a 'no obligation to buy' promise and a 'return to the shop if dissatisfied' guarantee on the front page.

Termination on demand – instantaneous, without mess, no counting losses or regrets – is the major advantage of internet dating. A reduction of the risks coupled with the avoidance of option-closing is what is left of rational choice in a world of fluid chances, shifting values and eminently unstable rules; and internet dating, unlike the awkward negotiation of mutual commitments, fulfils such new standards of rational choice perfectly (or near perfectly).

Shopping malls have done a lot to reclassify the labours of survival as entertainment and recreation. What used to be suffered and endured with a large admixture of resentment and repulsion under the intractable pressure of necessity has acquired the seductive powers of a promise of incalculable pleasures without incalculable risks attached. What shopping malls did for the chores of daily survival, internet dating has done for the negotiation of partnership. But just as the mitigation of necessity and the pressures of 'bare survival' was a necessary condition of the success of the shopping malls, internet dating would hardly have succeeded on its own unless it had been aided and abetted by the removal of full-time engagement, commitment and the obligation 'of being there for you whenever you need me' from the list of the necessary conditions of partnership.

Responsibility for deleting those conditions cannot be laid at the virtual door of electronic dating. Much else has happened on the road to liquid modern individualized society that has made long-term commitments thin on the ground, long-term engagement a rare expectation, and the obligation of mutual assistance 'come what may' a prospect that is neither realistic nor viewed as worthy of great effort.

The presumed key to everyone's happiness, and so the declared purpose of politics, is the increase of the gross national product (GNP). And GNP is measured by the amount of money spent by everyone together.

'Cut through the boosterism and hysterics,' write Jonathan Rowe and Judith Silverstein, 'and growth means simply "spending more money". It makes no difference where the money goes, and why.'[13]

In fact most of the money spent, and even more of the growth in spending, goes to finance the fight against consumer society's equivalent of 'iatrogenic ailments' – troubles caused by the boosting and then placating of yesterday's wants and fads. The American food industry spends some $21 billion annually on sowing and cultivating the desire for more sophisticated, outlandish and supposedly more tasty and exciting foods, while the diet and weight-loss industry earns $32 billion annually, and the outlays on medical treatment, in large part explained by the need to fight the bane of obesity, are expected to double over the next decade. Los Angeles residents pay on average $800 million a year to burn petrol, while hospitals admit record numbers of patients suffering from asthma, bronchitis and other breathing problems caused by air pollution, pushing to new heights their already record-breaking bill. As consuming (and spending) more than yesterday but (hopefully) not as much as tomorrow becomes the royal road to the solution of all social problems, and as the sky becomes the limit for the pulling power of successive consumer attractions, debt-collector companies, security firms and penitentiary outfits become major contributors to the growth of GNP. It is impossible to measure exactly the enormous and growing part played in pushing the GNP statistics upwards by the stress emitted by the liquid modern consumer's life-consuming preoccupations.

The accepted way of calculating 'national product' and its growth, and more particularly the fetish construed by current politics round the results of that calculation, rests on an assumption that is untested and seldom spelled out overtly, though it is widely contested whenever it is spelled out: that the sum total of human happiness grows as more money changes hands. In a market society, money changes hands on all sorts of occasions. To name but a few of the poignant examples collected by Jonathan Rowe,[14] money changes hands when someone becomes an invalid and the car is a wreck beyond repair as a result of a car accident; when lawyers step up their charges for seeing through a divorce case; or when people install water filters or switch to bottled water because the tap water is no longer drinkable. And so in all these and similar cases, 'national product' grows, and the ruling politicians along with the economists sitting on their brain trusts rejoice.

The GNP model that dominates (in fact, monopolizes) the fashion in which the denizens of a liquid modern, consumerist and individualized society think of welfare or of a 'good society' (on the rare occasions when they admit such thoughts into their concerns for a successful and happy life) is most remarkable not for what it misleadingly or downright wrongly classifies, but for what it does not classify at all; for what it leaves out of the calculation altogether, thereby denying it in practice any topical relevance to the issue of national wealth and collective and individual well-being.

Just as the all-ordering, all-classifying modern states could not suffer 'masterless men' and as the expanding, territory-greedy modern empires could not suffer 'no man's' lands – modern markets do not suffer gladly the 'non-market economy': the kind of life that reproduces itself without money changing hands.

For the theorists of the market economy, such life does not count – and therefore does not exist. For the practitioners of the market economy, it constitutes an offence and a challenge – a space not yet conquered, a standing invitation to invasion and conquest, a task not yet fulfilled which is clamouring for urgent action.

Reflecting the temporary nature of all and any *modus coexistendi* between the markets and a non-monetary economy, the theorists call the self-reproducing life or the self-reproducing fragments of life by names suggesting their abnormality and imminent demise. People who manage to produce the goods they need to sustain their mode of life, and so can do without regular visits to the shops, live 'from hand to mouth'; they lead a kind of existence that derives its meaning solely from what it lacks or misses – a primitive, miserable existence that precedes the 'economic take-off' with which *normal* life, needing no qualifiers, starts. Each instance of a good changing hands without money flowing in the opposite direction is relegated to the misty realm of the 'informal economy' – again the marked member of the opposition whose other, normal member (that is, money-mediated exchange) needs no denomination.

The practitioners of the market economy do whatever they can to reach the parts that the marketing experts have still failed to reach. The expansion is both horizontal and vertical, extensive and intensive: to be conquered are the lands still clinging to their 'hand to mouth' livelihood, but also the 'informal' economy's share of time in the lives of populations already converted to the shopping/consuming life. Non-monetary livelihoods need to be destroyed so that those who relied on them will have to face a

68

choice between shopping and starvation (not that, once having converted to shopping, they will be guaranteed to escape the famine). The areas of life not yet merchandized must be shown to hide dangers that cannot be staved off without the help of bought tools or services, or must be decried as inferior, repulsive and ultimately degrading. And decried they are.

What is most conspicuously missing in the economic calculus of the theorists, and figures at the top of the trade-war targets list composed by the practitioners of the market, is the huge area of what A. H. Halsey called the 'moral economy' – family sharing of goods and services, neighbourly help, friends' cooperation: all the motives, impulses and acts from which human bonds and lasting commitments are plaited.

The sole character the theorists regard as deserving of attention, because this is the one credited with 'keeping the economy on course' and lubricating the wheels of economic growth, is *homo oeconomicus* – the lonely, self-concerned and self-centred economic actor pursuing the best deal and guided by 'rational choice', careful not to fall prey to any emotions that defy translation into monetary gains, and populating a lifeworld full of other characters who share all those virtues but nothing else besides. The sole character the practitioners of the market are able and willing to recognize and accommodate is *homo consumens* – the lonely, self-concerned and self-centred shopper who has adopted the search for the best bargain as a cure for loneliness and knows of no other therapy; a character for whom the swarm of shopping-mall customers is the sole community known and needed; a character whose lifeworld is populated with other characters who share all those virtues but nothing else besides.

Der Mann ohne Eigenschaften – the man without qualities – of early modernity has matured into (or has he been crowded out by?) *der Mann ohne Verwandtschaften* – the man without bonds.

Homo oeconomicus and *homo consumens* are men and women *without social bonds*. They are the ideal residents of the market economy and the types that make the GNP watchers happy.

They are also fictions.

As one artificial barrier to free trade after another is broken and natural ones are eradicated and destroyed, the horizontal/extensive expansion of the market economy seems to be heading towards completion. But the vertical/intensive expansion is far from complete, and one wonders whether its completion is on the cards – or, indeed, conceivable at all.

It is thanks to the safety valve of the 'moral economy' that the tensions generated by the market economy stop short of acquiring explosive proportions. It is thanks to the cushion of the 'moral economy' that the human waste generated by the market economy stops short of becoming unmanageable. If it weren't for the corrective, mitigating, mellowing and compensating intervention of the moral economy, the market economy would expose its self-destructive drive. The daily miracle of the market economy's salvation/resurrection stems from its failure to follow that drive to its end.

Admitting only *homo oeconomicus* and *homo consumens* to the world ruled by the market economy makes a considerable number of humans ineligible for residence permits and allows few if any humans to enjoy lawful residence at all times and on all occasions. Few if any can escape the grey-painted area for which the market has no use and which it would be happy to excise and banish altogether from the world it rules.

What from the point of view of market conquest – already accomplished or still intended – is represented as a 'grey area' is for its conquered, partly conquered and designated to be conquered inhabitants a community, a neighbourhood, a circle of friends, partners in life and partners for life: a world where solidarity, compassion, sharing, mutual help and mutual sympathy (all notions alien to economic thought and abhorred by economic practice) suspend or elbow out rational choice and the pursuit of self-interest. A world whose residents are neither competitors nor objects of use and consumption, but fellows (helpers and helped) in the ongoing, never-ending joint effort of shared life-building and making shared life liveable.

The need for solidarity seems to withstand and survive market assaults – though not for the market's lack of trying. Where there is

70

a need, there is a chance of profit – and marketing experts stretch their ingenuity to the limit to suggest ways of buying solidarity, a friendly smile, togetherness or help-in-need in the shops. They constantly succeed – and constantly fail. Shop-supplied substitutes do not replace human bonds; in their shopping version, bonds turn into commodities; that is, they are transferred into another, market-ruled realm and cease to be the kinds of bonds that can satisfy the need for togetherness and that only in togetherness can be conceived and kept alive. The market's chase after untapped capital hidden in human sociality[15] cannot be won.

When looked at through the lenses of a properly constructed and smoothly functioning, orderly world, the 'grey area' of human solidarity, friendship and partnerships appears as the kingdom of _anarchy_.

The concept of 'anarchy' is burdened with its essentially anti-state history. From Godwin through Proudhon and Bakunin to Kropotkin, the theorists of anarchy and the founders of anarchist movements deployed the term 'anarchy' as a name of an alternative society and the antonym of a power-assisted, coercive order. The alternative society they postulated was to differ from the really existing one by the absence of the state – the epitome of inhuman, intrinsically corrupting power. Once the state power was dismantled and removed, human beings would resort (return?) to the assets of mutual help, using, as Mikhail Bakunin kept repeating, their naturally endowed capacity to think and to rebel.[16]

The wrath of the nineteenth-century anarchists focused on the state; the _modern_ state, to be precise, a novelty in their time and not solidly enough entrenched to claim traditional legitimacy or rely on routinized obedience. That state strove for meticulous and ubiquitous control over the aspects of human life which past powers had left to local collective ways and means. It claimed the right and devised means to interfere in areas from which past powers, however oppressive and exploitative, kept their distance. In particular, it set about dismantling _les pouvoirs intermediaires,_ that is the received forms of local autonomy, communal self-assertion and self-government. Under assault, the habitual ways of resolving problems and conflicts generated by joint living appeared to the pioneers of anarchic movements as unproblematically given and indeed 'natural'; they had also been imagined to be self-sustaining and fully capable of order maintenance under all social conditions and in all circumstances, so long as they were protected against impositions originating from the state. Anarchy, that is a society without a state and its coercive arms, was visualized as a non-coercive order, in which necessity did not clash with freedom nor freedom stand in the way of the prerequisites of living in company.

The early anarchist *Weltanschauung* had a pronounced nostalgic flavour which it shared with the utopian socialism of the time (Proudhon's and Weitling's teachings epitomizing their intimate affinity); a dream of retreat from the road entered with the birth of a new, modern form of social power and capitalism (that is, the separation of business from the household) – back to a romanticized rather than genuinely conflict-free cosiness of communal unity of feelings and deeds. It is in this early, nostalgic and utopian form that the idea of 'anarchy' settled in the awareness of modern society and in most of its political-science interpretations.

But there was another, less timebound meaning in anarchist thought, hiding behind its ostensive anti-state rebellion and for that reason only too easy to overlook. This other meaning is akin to that of Victor Turner's image of *communitas*:

> It is as though there are here two major 'models' for human interrelatedness, juxtaposed and alternating. The first is of society as a structured, differentiated, and often hierarchical system of politico-legal-economic positions...The second...is of society as an unstructured or rudimentarily structured and relatively undifferentiated *communitas*, community, or even communion of equal individuals who submit together to the general authority of the ritual elders.[17]

Turner used the language of anthropology and located the issue of *communitas* within the customary anthropological problematics, concerned as it were with the differences between the ways in which human aggregates ('societies', 'cultures') secured their durability and continuous self-reproduction. But the two models that Turner described may be also interpreted as representations of complementary modes of human coexistence that mix in varying proportions in every and any lasting human aggregate, rather than of different types of societies.

No variety of human togetherness is fully structured, no internal differentiation is all-embracing, comprehensive and free from ambivalence, no hierarchy is total and frozen. The logic of categories ill fits the endemic variegation and messiness of human interactions. Each attempt at complete structuration leaves numerous 'loose strings' and contentious meanings; each produces its blank spots, underdefined areas, ambiguities and 'no man's' territories lacking their official ordnance surveys and maps. All such leftovers of the effort to bring order constitute the domain of human spontaneity, experimentation and self-constitution. *Communitas* is, for better or worse, a lining of every *societas* cloud – and in its absence (were such absence conceivable) that cloud would disperse – *societas* would fall apart at its seams. It is *societas* with its routine and *communitas* with its anarchy that *together*, in their reluctant and conflict-ridden cooperation, make the difference between order and chaos.

The task which institutionalization, flexing its coercive arms, botched or failed to accomplish is left to the spontaneous inventiveness of human beings to repair or complete. Denied the comfort of the routine, creativity (as Bakunin pointed out) has only two human faculties to rely on: the ability to think, and the inclination (and courage) to rebel. The exercise of either of these two faculties is pregnant with risk; and, unlike in the case of institutionally entrenched and protected routine, not much can be done to minimize that risk, let alone to eliminate it. *Communitas* (not to be confused with the countersocieties claiming the name of 'community' yet busy emulating the ways and means of *societas*) inhabits the land of uncertainty – and would not survive in any other country.

The survival and well-being of *communitas* (and so, indirectly, of *societas* as well) depend on human imagination, inventiveness and courage in *breaking* the routine and trying the *untried* ways. They depend, in other words, on the human ability to live with risk and accept responsibility for the consequences. It is these abilities that are the supports for the 'moral economy' – mutual care and help, living *for* the other, weaving the tissue of human commitments, fastening and servicing interhuman bonds, translating rights into obligations, sharing responsibility for everyone's fortune and welfare – indispensable for plugging the holes pierced and stemming the floods released by the forever inconclusive enterprise of structuration.

The invasion and colonization of *communitas*, the site of the moral economy, by consumer market forces constitutes the most awesome of dangers threatening the present form of human togetherness.

The principal targets of the assault by the market are humans as *producers*; in a fully conquered and colonized land, only human *consumers* would be issued residence permits. The diffuse cottage industry of shared life conditions would be put out of operation and dismantled. Forms of life, and the partnerships that support them, would be available only in the shape of commodities. The order-obsessed state fought (at its own peril) anarchy, that trademark of *communitas*, because of the threat to power-assisted routine; the profit-obsessed consumer market fights that anarchy because of its obstreperous productive capacity, as well as the potential for self-sufficiency it suspects will grow out of it. It is because the moral economy has little need of the market that market forces are up in arms against it.

A twofold strategy is deployed in that war.

First, as many aspects as possible of the market-independent moral economy are commodified and recast as aspects of consumption.

Second, anything in the moral economy of the *communitas* that resists such commodification is denied relevance to the prosperity of the society of consumers; it is stripped of value in a society trained to measure values in currency and to identify them with the price tags carried by sellable and purchasable objects and services; and ultimately it is pressed out of public (and, it is hoped, individual) attention by being struck out of the public accounts of human well-being.

The outcome of the present war is anything but a foregone conclusion, though thus far there seems to be only one side on the offensive, with the other side in an almost continuous retreat. *Communitas* has lost a lot of ground; trading-posts hoping to grow into shopping malls are cropping up on the fields it once cultivated.

Loss of territory is an ominous and potentially disastrous development in every war, but the factor that ultimately decides the outcome of hostilities is the fighting ability of the troops. Lost territory is easier to recoup than a loss of fighting spirit and a fading of trust in the purpose and chances of resistance. More than anything else, it is the second development that portends ill for the fate of the moral economy.

The major and probably the most seminal success of the market offensive so far has been the gradual (and by no means complete and unredeemable) but persistent crumbling away of the skills of sociality. In matters of interpersonal relations, the deskilled actors find themselves ever more often in 'agentic mode' – acting heteronomously, on overt or subliminal instructions, and guided primarily by the wish to follow the briefings to the letter and by the fear of departing from the models currently in vogue. The seductive allure of heteronomous action consists mostly in a surrender of responsibility; an authoritative recipe is purchased in a package deal with a release from the need to answer for the adverse results of its application.

The fading of sociality skills is boosted and accelerated by the tendency, inspired by the dominant consumerist life mode, to treat other humans as objects of consumption and to judge them after the pattern of consumer objects by the volume of pleasure they are likely to offer, and in 'value for money' terms. At best, the others are valued as companions-in-the-essentially-solitary-activity of consumption; fellows in the joys of consumption, whose presence and active participation may intensify those pleasures. In the process, the intrinsic value of others as unique human beings (and so also the concern with others for their own, and that uniqueness's, sake) has been all but lost from sight. Human solidarity is the first casualty of the triumphs of the consumer market.

3

On the Difficulty of Loving
Thy Neighbour

The call to 'love thy neighbour as thyself', says Freud (in *Civiliza-tion and its Discontents*),[1] is one of the fundamental precepts of civilized life. It is also the most contrary to the kind of reason that civilization promotes: the reason of self-interest, and of the pursuit of happiness. The founding precept of civilization may only be accepted as 'making sense', and embraced and practised, if one surrenders to the theological admonition *credere quia absurdum –* believe it because it is absurd.

Indeed, it is enough to ask 'why should I do it? What good will it do to me?' to feel the absurdity of the demand to love one's neighbour – any neighbour, for the sole reason of being a neigh-bour. If I love someone, she or he must have deserved it in some way... 'They deserve it if they are so much like me in so many important ways that I can love myself in them; and they deserve it if they are so much more perfect than myself that I can love in them the ideal of my own self... But if he is a stranger to me and if he cannot attract me by any worth of his own or any significance that he may already have acquired for my emotional life, it will be hard for me to love him.' The demand feels yet more irksome and inane since all too often I cannot find much evidence that the stranger whom I am supposed to love loves me or even shows me 'the slightest consideration. When it suits him, he would not hesitate to injure me, jeer at me, slander me and show me his superior power...'

And so, Freud asks, 'what is the point of a precept enunciated with so much solemnity if its fulfilment cannot be recommended as reasonable?' Seeking an answer, one is tempted to conclude, against good sense, that 'love your neighbour' is 'a commandment which is really justified by the fact that nothing else runs as strongly counter to the original nature of man'. The less likely a norm is to be obeyed, the more the obstinacy with which it is likely to be restated. And the injunction to love one's neighbour is perhaps less likely to be obeyed than any other norm. When the Talmudic sage Rabbi Hillel was challenged by a prospective convert to explain God's teaching in the time the challenger could stand on one foot, he offered 'love thy neighbour as thyself' as the only, yet complete, answer, encapsulating the totality of God's injunctions. Accepting such a command is a leap of faith; a decisive leap, through which a human being breaks out of the carapace of 'natural' drives, urges and predilections, takes a position away from and against nature, and turns into the 'unnatural' being that, unlike the beasts (and indeed the angels, as Aristotle pointed out), humans are.

Accepting the precept of loving one's neighbour is the birth act of humanity. All other routines of human cohabitation, as well as their predesigned or retrospectively discovered rules, are but a (never complete) list of footnotes to that precept. Were this precept to be ignored or thrown away, there would be no one to make that list or ponder its completeness.

Loving your neighbour may require a leap of faith; the result, though, is the birth act of humanity. It is also the fateful passage from the instinct of survival to morality.

This is a passage that renders morality a part, perhaps a *conditio sine qua non*, of survival. With that ingredient, survival of *a human* becomes the survival of *humanity* in the human.

'Love thy neighbour as thyself' implicitly casts self-love as unproblematically given, as always-already-there. Self-love is a matter of survival, and survival needs no commandments, since other (non-human) living creatures do very well without them, thank you. Loving one's neighbour as one loves oneself makes *human* survival unlike the survival of any other living creatures. Without that extension/transcendence of self-love, the prolongation of physical, bodily life is not yet, by itself, a *human* survival; is not the kind of survival that sets the humans apart from the beasts (and – never forget it – the angels). The precept to love one's neighbour challenges and defies the instincts set by nature; but it also challenges and defies the meaning of survival set by nature, and of that self-love which protects it.

Loving your neighbour may not be a staple product of the survival instinct – but nor is your self-love, picked as the model of neighbourly love, such a product.

Self-love – what does that mean? What do I love 'in myself'? What do I love when I love myself? We, humans, share survival instincts with our near, not so near and quite distant animal cousins – but when it comes to self-love, our roads part and we are on our own.

It is true that self-love prompts us to 'stick to life', to try hard to stay alive for better or worse, to resist and fight back against whatever may threaten the premature or abrupt termination of life, and to protect, or better still beef up our fitness and vigour to make that resistance effective. In this, however, our animal cousins are masters that are no less accomplished and seasoned than the most dedicated and artful fitness addicts and health fiends among us. Our animal cousins (except the 'domesticated' among them, whom we, their human masters, have managed to strip of their natural endowments so that they can better serve our, rather than their, survival) need no expert counsellors to tell them how to stay alive and keep fit. Nor do they need self-love to instruct them that staying alive and fit is the right thing to do.

Survival (animal survival, physical, bodily survival) can do without self-love. As a matter of fact, it may do better without it than in its company! The roads of the survival instincts and of self-love may run parallel, but they may also run in opposite directions... Self-love may rebel *against* the continuation of life. Self-love may prompt us to *invite* the danger and to welcome the threat. Self-love can prod us to *reject* a life that is not up to our love's standards and therefore unworthy of living.

Because what we love in our self-love is the selves fit to be loved. What we love is the state, or the hope, of being loved. Of being *objects worthy of love*, being *recognized* as such, and given the *proof* of that recognition.

In short: in order to have self-love, we need to be loved. Refusal of love – denial of the status of a love-worthy object – breeds self-hatred. Self-love is built out of the love offered to us by others. If substitutes are used for its construction, they must be likenesses, however fraudulent, of such love. Others must love us first, so that we can begin to love ourselves.

And how do we know that we have not been snubbed or dumped as a hopeless case, that love is, may be, will be forthcoming, that we are worthy of it and so have the right to indulge in, and relish, *amour de soi*? We know it, we believe that we know it, and we are reassured that the belief is not mistaken, when we are talked to and listened to. When we are listened to attentively, with an interest that betrays/signals a readiness to respond. We gather then that we are *respected*. We suppose, that is, that what we think, do, or intend to do – counts.

If others respect me, then obviously there must be 'in me', must there not, something that only I can offer to others; and obviously there are such others, aren't there, who would be glad to be offered it and grateful if they were. I am important, and what I think and say and do is important as well. I am not a cipher, easily replaced and disposed of. I 'make a difference' to more than myself. What I say and what I am and do matters – and this is not just my flight of fancy. Whatever there is in the world around me, that world would be poorer, less interesting and less promising were I suddenly to cease to exist or go elsewhere.

If this is what makes us right and proper objects of self-love, then the call to 'love our neighbours as ourselves' (that is, to expect the neighbours to wish to be loved for the same reasons that prompt our self-love) invokes the neighbours' desire to have their dignity of bearing a unique, irreplaceable and non-disposable

80

value recognized, admitted and confirmed. That call prods us to assume that the neighbours do indeed represent such values – at least until proven otherwise. Loving our neighbours as we love ourselves would mean then *respecting each other's uniqueness* – the value of our differences that enrich the world we jointly inhabit and so make it more fascinating and enjoyable a place and add further to the cornucopia of its promises.

In a scene in Andrzej Wajda's most human of films – *Korczak* – Janusz Korczak (pen name of the great pedagogue born Henryk Goldszmit), a most human film hero, is reminded of the horrors of wars waged in the lifetime of his much suffering generation. He remembers those atrocities, of course, and deeply resents and abhors them as such acts of inhumanity deserve to be resented and ought be abhorred. And yet most vividly, and with the greatest horror, he remembers a drunken man kicking a child.

In our world obsessed with statistics, averages and majorities we tend to measure the degree of the inhumanity of wars by the number of their casualties. We tend to measure the evil, the cruelty, the offensiveness and the infamy of victimization by the number of its victims. But in 1944, in the midst of the most murderous of wars ever waged by human beings, Ludwig Wittgenstein noted:

No cry of torment can be greater than the cry of one man.
Or again, *no* torment can be greater than what a single human being may suffer.
The whole planet can suffer no greater torment than a *single* soul.

Half a century later, when pressed by Leslie Stahl of CBS television about half a million children who died because of the US's continuous military blockade of Iraq, Madeleine Albright, then US ambassador to the United Nations, did not deny the charge and admitted that 'this was a difficult choice to take'. But she justified that choice: 'we think that the price was worth paying.'

Albright, let us be fair, neither was nor is alone in following that kind of reasoning. 'You cannot make an omelette without breaking eggs' is the favourite excuse of the visionaries, the spokespeople for the officially endorsed visions, and the generals acting on the spokespeople's behest alike. That formula has turned over the years into a veritable motto of our brave modern times.

Whoever those 'we' are who 'think' and in whose name Albright spoke, it is exactly the cold cruelty of their kind of judgement which Wittgenstein opposed and by which Korczak was shocked, outraged and revolted, resolving to make a whole life out of that revulsion.

Most of us would agree that senseless suffering and senselessly inflicted pain can have no excuse and would not be defensible in any court; but fewer are prepared to admit that to starve or cause death to just one human being is not, cannot be, a 'price worth paying', however 'sensible' or even noble the cause may be for which payment is made. Neither humiliation nor denial of human dignity can be such a price. It is not only that the dignified life and respect due to the humanity of each human being combine into a supreme value that cannot be outweighed or compensated for by any volume or any amount of other values, but *all other values are values only in as far as they serve human dignity and promote its cause.* All things valuable in human life are but so many different tokens to purchase that single value that makes life worth living. The one who seeks survival by murdering humanity in other human beings survives the death of his own humanity.

Denial of human dignity discredits the worth of any cause that needs such denial to assert itself. And the suffering of just one child discredits that worth as radically and completely as does the suffering of millions. What may be true for omelettes becomes a cruel lie when applied to human happiness and well-being.

It is commonly accepted by Korczak's biographers and disciples that the key to his thoughts and deeds was his love of children. Such an interpretation is well grounded; Korczak's love of children was passionate and unconditional, complete and all-embracing – enough to sustain a whole life of uniquely cohesive sense and integrity. And yet, like most interpretations, this one stops short of the completeness of its object.

Korczak loved children as few of us are ready or able to love, but *what he loved in children was their humanity.* Humanity at its best

– undistorted, untruncated, untrimmed and unmaimed, whole in its childish inchoateness and nascence, full of as-yet-unbetrayed promise and as-yet-uncompromised potential. The world into which the potential carriers of humanity are born and in which they grow is known to be more adept at clipping wings than prompting the would-be flyers to spread them, and so in Korczak's opinion it was only in children that humanity could be found, caught and preserved (for a time, only for a time!) pristine and whole.

It would perhaps be better to change the world's ways and make the human habitat more hospitable to human dignity, so that coming of age would not require the compromising of a child's humanity. Young Henryk Goldszmit shared in the hopes of the century in which he was born and believed that changing the world's abominable habits *was* in the power of humans: a task both feasible and bound to be attained. But as times went by, as the stacks of the victims and the 'collateral damage' of ill intentions as much as of noble intentions mounted sky-high, and as the necrosis and putridity of the flesh into which dreams tended to turn left less and less to the imagination, such elevated hopes were plucked of their credibility. Janusz Korczak knew all too well the uncomfortable truth of which Henryk Goldszmit was all but ignorant: there can be no shortcuts leading to a world made to the measure of human dignity, while the 'really existing world' constructed daily by people already shorn of their dignity and unused to respecting human dignity in others is unlikely ever to be remade to that measure.

For this world of ours you cannot legislate perfection. You cannot force virtue on the world, but neither can you persuade the world to behave virtuously. You cannot make this world kind and considerate to the human beings who inhabit it, and as accommodating to their dreams of dignity as you would ideally wish it to be. *But you must try.* You will try. You would, at any rate, if you were that Janusz Korczak who grew out of Henryk Goldszmit.

But how would you try? A little like the old-style utopian visionaries who – having failed to square the circle of security and freedom in the Big Society – turned into the designers of gated communities, shopping malls and theme parks ... In your case, by protecting the dignity with which every human is born against the thieves and the forgers scheming to steal it or to twist and maim it; and you'd start on that lifelong job of protection when there is still time, during that dignity's childhood years. You would try to lock the stable *before* the horse has bolted or been stolen.

One, and apparently the most reasonable, way of doing this is to shelter children from the poisonous effluvia of a world tainted and corrupted by human humiliation and indignity; to bar access to the law of the jungle that starts just on the other side of the shelter's door. When his orphanage moved from its prewar Krochmalna location to the Warsaw Ghetto, Korczak ordered that the entry door be permanently locked and the ground-floor windows bricked up. As the imminent deportations to gas chambers were turning into a certainty, Korczak reputedly opposed the idea of closing the orphanage and sending children out to seek individually a chance of escape which some might (just might) find. He might have reckoned that the chance was not worth taking: once out of their shelter, the children would learn fear, abasement and hatred. They would lose the most precious of values – their dignity. Once robbed of that value, what point would there be in staying alive? The value, the most precious of human values, the *sine qua non* attribute of humanity, is a life of dignity; not survival at all costs.

Spielberg could learn something from Korczak – the man, and *Korczak* the film.

Something that he did not know, or did not wish to know, or did not wish to admit that he knew; something about human life and about such values as make that life worth living; something of which he displayed ignorance or disregard in his own narrative of inhumanity, the box-office record-breaking *Schindler's List*, to the applause of our world that has little use for dignity but much demand for humiliation, and that came to see the purpose of life as outliving others.

The film *Schindler's List* is about outliving others; surviving at all costs and in whatever condition, come what may, doing what needs to be done. The densely packed movie theatre bursts into applause when Schindler manages to get his master of works out of the train ready to go to Treblinka; never mind that the train has not been stopped and the rest of the passengers in the cattle carriages will end their journey in the gas chambers. And the applause comes again when Schindler refuses the offer of 'other Jewesses' to replace '*his* Jewesses' 'wrongly' marked for the crematoria, and manages to 'correct' 'the mistake'.

The right of the stronger, more astute, artful or cunning to do whatever they can contrive to outlive the weaker and the hapless is one of the most horrifying lessons of the Holocaust.

A gruesome, frightening lesson, but no less eagerly learned, appropriated, memorized and applied for this reason. To be fit for adoption, that lesson must first be thoroughly stripped of all ethical connotations, right to the bare bones of a zero-sum game of survival. Life is about survival. The stronger lives. Who strikes first, survives. As long as you are the stronger, you may get away, unpunished, with whatever you have done to the weak. The fact that the dehumanization of the victims dehumanizes – morally devastates – their victimizers is dismissed as a minor irritant; that is, if it has not been passed over in silence. What counts is to get on top and to stay on top. Surviving – staying alive – is a value apparently unscathed and untarnished by the inhumanity of a life dedicated to survival. It is worth pursuing for its own sake, however high are the costs paid by the defeated and however deeply and beyond repair this may deprave and degrade the victors.

This terrifying and most inhuman among the Holocaust's lessons comes complete with an inventory of the pains one may inflict on the weak in order to assert one's own strength. Rounding up, deporting, locking in concentration camps or bringing the plight of whole populations close to the concentration camp model, demonstrating the futility of the law through executing suspects on the spot, imprisoning without trial and term of confinement, spreading the terror which random and haphazardly inflicted punishment spawns, all these have been amply proved to serve effectively the cause of survival and so to be 'rational'.

The list may be, and is, extended as the time goes by. 'New and improved' expedients are tried and, if successfully tested, are added to the inventory – like razing single homes or whole residential districts, uprooting olive groves, burning or ploughing up crops, setting fire to workplaces and otherwise destroying sources of already miserable livelihoods. All such measures display a propensity to be self-propelling and self-exacerbating. As the list of atrocities committed grows, so does the need to apply them ever more resolutely to prevent the victims from making their voices not just heard but also listened to. And as old stratagems become routine and the horror they have sown among their targets wears off, new and more painful and horrifying contrivances need to be feverishly sought.

Victimization hardly ever humanizes its victims. Being a victim does not guarantee a seat on the moral high ground.

In a private letter objecting to my consideration of the possibility of cutting the 'schismogenetic chain' that tends to transform victims into victimizers, Antonina Zhelazkova, the intrepid and uniquely perceptive ethnologist and dedicated explorer of the Balkans' apparently bottomless powder-keg of ethnic and any other animosities, wrote:

> I do not accept that people are in a position to fight the urge of being killers after they were victims. You demand too much from the common people. It is usual for the victim to turn into a butcher. The poor man, as well as the poor in spirit whom you have helped, come to hate you . . . because they want to forget the past, the humiliation, the pain and the fact that they had achieved something with someone's help, out of someone's pity but not alone . . . How to escape from the pain and humiliation – the natural thing is by killing or humiliating your executioner or benefactor. Or, by finding another, weaker person in order to triumph over him.

Let us beware dismissing Zhelazkova's warning lightly. The odds against common humanity seem indeed overwhelming. The weapons do not speak, while the sound of humans speaking seems to be an abominably weak response to the whizz of missiles and the deafening racket of explosives.

Memory is a mixed blessing. More precisely, it is a blessing and a curse rolled into one. It may 'keep alive' many things, of sharply unequal value for the group and its neighbours. The past is a bagful of events, and memory never retains them all, and whatever it retains or recovers from oblivion it never reproduces in its 'pristine' form (whatever that may mean). The 'whole past', and the past 'wie es ist eigentlich gewesen' (as Ranke suggested it should be retold by the historians) is never recaptured by memory; and if it were, memory would be a straightforward liability rather than an asset to the living. Memory *selects*, and *interprets* – and *what* is to be selected and *how* it needs to be interpreted is a moot matter and an object of continuous contention. The resurrection of the past, keeping the past alive, can only be attained through the active, choosing, reprocessing and recycling, work of memory.

In *The Ethical Demand*, Løgstrup vented a more optimistic view of the natural inclination of humans.

'It is a characteristic of human life that we normally encounter one another with natural trust,' he wrote then. 'Only because of some special circumstance do we ever distrust a stranger in advance...Under normal circumstances, however, we accept the stranger's word and do not mistrust him until we have some particular reason to do so. We never suspect a person of falsehood until after we have caught him in a lie.'[2]

The Ethical Demand was conceived by Løgstrup during the eight years following his marriage to Rosalie Maria Pauly, spent in the small and peaceful parish of Funen Island. With due respect to the friendly and sociable residents of Aarhus where Løgstrup was to spend the rest of his life teaching theology in the local university, I doubt whether such ideas could gestate in his mind once he had settled in that town and faced point-blank the realities of the world at war and under occupation, as an active member of the Danish resistance.

People tend to weave their images of the world out of the yarn of their experience. The present generation may find the sunny and buoyant image of a trusting and trustworthy world far-fetched – sharply at odds with what they themselves learn daily and what is insinuated by the common narratives of human experience and recommended life strategies they hear daily. They would rather recognize themselves in the acts and confessions of the characters in the recent wave of avidly watched, hugely popular television shows of the *Big Brother, Survivor* and *The Weakest Link* type. They convey a quite different message: a stranger is *not* to be trusted. The *Survivor* series bears a subtitle that tells it all: 'Trust no one.' Fans and addicts of the 'reality TV' shows would reverse Løgstrup's verdict: 'It is a characteristic of human life that we normally encounter one another with natural suspicion.'

These TV spectacles that took millions of viewers by storm and immediately captured their imagination were public rehearsals of the *disposability* of humans. They carried an indulgence and a warning rolled into one story, their message being that no one is indispensable, no one has the right to his or her share in the fruits of joint effort just because he or she has added at some point to their growth; let alone because of being, simply, a member of the team. Life is a hard game for hard people, so the message went. Each game starts from scratch, past merits do not count, you are worth only as much as the results of your last duel. Each player at every moment is only for herself (or himself), and to progress, not to mention reach the top, one must first cooperate in excluding those many others eager to survive and succeed who block the way – but only to outwit, one by one, all those with whom one used to cooperate, and leave them – defeated and no longer useful – behind.

The others are, first and foremost, competitors; scheming as all competitors do, digging holes, laying ambushes, itching for us to stumble and fall. The assets that help the victors to outlast the competition and thus to emerge victorious from the cut-throat battle are of many sorts, ranging from blatant self-assertiveness to meek self-effacement. And yet whatever stratagem is deployed and whatever the assets of the survivors and the liabilities of the defeated, the story of survival is bound to develop in the same monotonous way: *in a game of survival, trust, compassion and mercy* (the paramount attributes of Løgstrup's 'sovereign expression of life') *are suicidal*. If you are not tougher and less scrupulous than all the others, you will be done in by them, with or without remorse. We are back to the sombre truth of the Darwinian world: it is the fittest who invariably survive. Or, rather, survival is the ultimate proof of fitness.

Were the young people of our times readers of books, and particularly of old books not currently on the bestseller list, they would be more likely to agree with the bitter, not at all sunny picture of the world painted by the Russian exile and Sorbonne philosopher, Leon Shestov: '*Homo homini lupus* is one of the most steadfast maxims of eternal morality. In each of our neighbours we fear a wolf...We are so poor, so weak, so easily ruined and destroyed! How can we help being afraid!...We see danger, danger only...'[3] They would insist, as Shestov did and as the *Big Brother* shows promoted to the rank of common sense, that this is a tough world, meant for tough people: a world of individuals left to rely solely on their own cunning, trying to outwit and outdo each other. Meeting a stranger you need vigilance first, and vigilance second and third. Coming together, standing shoulder to shoulder and working in teams make a lot of sense as long as they help you to get your own way; there is no reason why they should last once they bring no more benefit, or bring less benefit than shedding the commitments and cancelling the obligations hopefully, or just possibly, would.

Young people born, growing and coming of age at the turn of the century would also find familiar, perhaps even self-evident, Anthony Giddens's description of the 'pure relationship'.[4]

The 'pure relationship' tends to be the prevailing form of human togetherness today, entered 'for what can be derived by each person' and 'continued only in so far as it is thought by both parties to deliver enough satisfactions for each individual to stay within it'.

The present-day 'pure relationship', in Giddens's description, is

not, as marriage once was, a 'natural condition' whose durability can be taken for granted short of certain extreme circumstances. It is a feature of the pure relationship that it can be terminated, more or less at will, by either partner at any particular point. For a relationship to stand a chance of lasting, commitment is necessary; yet anyone who commits herself without reservations risks great hurt in the future, should the relationship become dissolved.

Commitment to another person or persons, particularly an unconditional commitment and most certainly a 'till death us do part', for better and worse and for richer and poorer kind of commitment, looks ever more like a trap that needs to be avoided at all costs.

About something they approve of, young people say 'it is cool.' An apt word: whatever other features human acts and interactions might have, interaction should not be allowed to warm up and particularly stay warm; it is OK as long as it stays cool, and being cool means being OK. If you know that your partner may opt out at any moment, with or without your agreement (as soon as they find that you, as the source of their enjoyment, have been emptied of your potential, holding little promise of new joys, or just because the grass appears greener on the other side of the fence), investing your feelings into the current relationship is always a risky step. Investing strong feelings in your partnership and taking an oath of allegiance means taking an enormous risk: it makes you *dependent* on your partner (though let us note that dependency, now fast becoming a derogatory term, is what the moral responsibility for the Other is all about – for Løgstrup as much as for Levinas).

To rub salt into the wound, your dependency – due to the 'purity' of your relationship – may not and need not be reciprocated. Therefore *you* are bound, but *your partner* is free to go, and no kind of bond that may keep you in place is enough to make sure that they won't. The widely shared, indeed commonplace awareness that all relationships are 'pure' (that is: frail, fissiparous, unlikely to last longer than the convenience they bring, and so always 'until further notice') is hardly a soil in which trust may take root and blossom.

Loose and eminently revocable partnerships have replaced the model of a 'till death us do part' personal union that still held, for better or worse (even if showing a growing number of off-putting cracks), at the time when Løgstrup recorded his belief in the 'naturalness' and the 'normality' of trust, and announced his verdict that it was the *suspension or cancellation* of trust, rather than its *unconditional and spontaneous gift*, that was an exception caused by extraordinary circumstances and therefore requiring an explanation.

The frailty, sickliness, and vulnerability of personal partnerships are not however the only features of the present-day life setting that sap the credibility of Løgstrup's suppositions. An unprecedented fluidity, fragility and in-built transience (the famed 'flexibility') mark all sorts of social bonds which but a few dozen years ago combined into a durable, reliable framework inside which a web of human interactions could be securely woven. They affect particularly, and perhaps most seminally, employment and professional relations. With skills falling out of demand in less time than it takes to acquire and master them, with educational credentials losing value against their cost of purchase by the year or even turning into 'negative equity' long before their allegedly lifelong 'sell-by' date, with places of work disappearing with little or no warning, and with the course of life sliced into a series of ever shorter one-off projects, life prospects look increasingly like the haphazard convolutions of smart rockets in search of elusive, ephemeral and restless targets, rather than a predesigned and predetermined, predictable trajectory of a ballistic missile.

The world today seems to be conspiring against trust.

Trust may remain, as Knud Løgstrup suggest, a natural outpouring of the 'sovereign expression of life', but once emitted it now seeks in vain a place to anchor. Trust has been sentenced to a life full of frustration. People (singly, severally, or conjointly), companies, parties, communities, great causes or the life patterns invested with authority to guide one's life fail all too often to repay devotion. Anyway, they are seldom paragons of consistency and long-term continuity. There is hardly a single reference point on which attention can be reliably and securely fixed, so that the beguiled guidance-seekers can be absolved from the irksome duty of constant vigilance and incessant retractions of steps taken or intended. No orientation points are available that seem to have a longer life expectation than the orientation-seekers themselves, however abominably short their own corporeal lives might be. Individual experience stubbornly points to the self as the most likely pivot of the duration and continuity so avidly sought.

In our society allegedly addicted to reflection, trust is unlikely to receive much reinforcement. A sober scrutiny of the data supplied by life's evidence points in the opposite direction, repeatedly revealing the perpetual fickleness of rules and the frailty of bonds. Does this mean, however, that Løgstrup's decision to invest hopes of morality in the spontaneous, *endemic tendency* to trust others has been invalidated by the *endemic uncertainty* saturating the world of our time?

One would be entitled to say so – if not for the fact that it was never Løgstrup's view that moral impulses arise out of reflection. On the contrary: in his view, the hope of morality was vested precisely in its *prereflexive spontaneity*: 'Mercy is spontaneous because the least interruption, the least calculation, the least dilution of it in order to serve something else destroys it entirely, indeed turns it into the opposite of what it is, unmercifulness.'[5]

Emmanuel Levinas is known to insist that the question 'why should I be moral?' (that is, asking for arguments of the kind 'what is there in it for me?', 'what did that person do for me to justify my care?', 'why should I care if so many others do not?', or 'could not someone else do it instead of me?') is not the *starting point* of moral conduct, but a signal of its *decease*; just as all amorality began with Cain's question, 'Am I my brother's keeper?' Løgstrup seems to agree.

'The *need* for morality' (that expression is already an oxymoron; whatever answers a 'need' is something other than morality) or just 'the advisability of morality' cannot be discursively established, let alone proved. Morality is nothing but an innately prompted manifestation of humanity – it does not 'serve' any 'purpose' and most surely is not guided by the expectation of profit, comfort, glory or self-enhancement. It is true that objectively good – helpful and useful – deeds have time and again been performed out of the actor's calculation of gain, be it to earn

Divine grace, to purchase public esteem or to ensure absolution from mercilessness shown on other occasions; these, however, cannot be classified as genuinely *moral* acts precisely because of having been so *motivated*.

In moral acts, an 'ulterior motive is ruled out', Løgstrup insists. The spontaneous expression of life is *radical* precisely thanks to 'the absence of ulterior motives' – both amoral and *moral*. This is one more reason why the ethical demand, that 'objective' pressure to be moral emanating from the very fact of being alive and sharing the planet with others, is and must stay silent. Since 'obedience to the ethical demand' can easily turn (be deformed and distorted) into a motive for conduct, the ethical demand is at its best when it is forgotten and not thought of: its radicalness 'consists in its demanding that it be superfluous'.[6] 'Immediacy of human contact is sustained by the immediate expressions of life'[7] and it needs, or indeed tolerates, no other supports.

In practical terms, it means that however much a human being may resent being left alone (in the last account) to his or her own counsel and responsibility, it is precisely that loneliness that contains a hope of a morally impregnated togetherness. Hope; not certainty.

Spontaneity and sovereignty of expressions of life do not vouch for the resulting conduct being the ethically proper and laudable choice between good and evil. The point is, though, that blunders *and* right choices arise from the same condition – as do the craven impulses to run for cover that authoritative commands obligingly provide *and* the boldness to accept responsibility. Without bracing oneself for the possibility of making wrong choices, there is hardly a way to persevere in the search for the right choice. Far from being a major threat to morality (and so an abomination to ethical philosophers), *uncertainty is the home ground of the moral person and the only soil out of which morality can spring shoots and flourish.*

But, as Løgstrup rightly points out, it is the 'immediacy of human contact' that is 'sustained by the immediate expressions of life'. I presume that the connection and the mutual conditioning act both ways. 'Immediacy' seems to play a role in Løgstrup's thinking similar to 'proximity' in Levinas's writings. 'Immediate expressions of life' are triggered by proximity, or by the immediate presence of the other human being – weak and vulnerable, suffering and needing help. We are challenged by what we see; and we are challenged to act – to help, to defend, to bring solace, to cure or save.

'The sovereign expression of life' is another 'brute fact' – just like Levinas's 'responsibility', or indeed Løgstrup's own 'ethical demand'.

Unlike the ethical demand, perpetually in waiting, inaudible, unexhausted, unfulfilled and perhaps forever, in principle, unfulfillable and inexhaustible – the sovereign expression of life is however always already fulfilled and complete; though not by choice, but 'spontaneously, without being demanded'.[8] It is, we may assume, that 'no choice' status of expressions of life that explains the ascription of 'sovereignty'.

'The sovereign expression of life' may be seen as another name for Martin Heidegger's *Befindlichkeit* (being situated, an essentially ontological notion) combined with *Stimmung* (being tuned, the epistemological reflex of 'being situated').[9] As Heidegger intimated, before any choosing can start, we are already immersed in the world and tuned to that immersion – armed with *Vorurteil, Vorhabe, Vorsicht, Vorgriff*, all those capacities with the 'vor' ('pre-') prefix that precede all knowledge and constitute its very possibility. But Heideggerian *Stimmung* is intimately related to *das Man* – that 'nobody, to whom all our existence... has already surrendered'. 'At the beginning, I am not "me" in the sense of my own self; to start with, being is *Man* and tends to remain so.' Such a state of 'Being as *das Man*' is in its essence the state of conformity *an sich*, conformity unaware of itself as conformity (and thus not to be confused with the sovereign choice of solidarity). As long as it appears in the guise of *das Man, Mitsein* ('Being With') is a fate, not a destiny nor a vocation. And so is the conformity of the surrender to *das Man*: it needs first to be unmasked as conformity before it can be either rejected and fought back against in the critical act of self-assertion, or wholeheartedly embraced as a life strategy and life purpose.

On the one hand, by insisting on its 'spontaneity' Løgstrup suggests such '*an sich*' status for life expressions, reminiscent of that of *Befindlichkeit* and *Stimmung*. On the other hand, however, he seems to identify the sovereign expression of life with the *rejection* of that primeval, 'naturally given' conformity (he strongly objects to the 'absorption' of sovereign expressions by conformity, their 'drowning in a life where one individual imitates another'), though he would not identify them either with the original act of the self's emancipation, of breaking through the protective shield of the *an sich* status. He insists that 'it is not a foregone conclusion that the sovereign expression of life will prevail.'[10]

Sovereign expression has a powerful adversary – the 'constrained' expression, an expression externally induced, and so heteronomous instead of autonomous; or rather (in an interpretation probably more attuned to Løgstrup's intention) an expression whose motives (once re-presented, or rather misrepresented, as *causes*) are projected upon the outside agents.

Examples of the 'constrained' expression are named as offence, jealousy and envy. In each case, a striking feature of conduct is the self-deception aimed at disguising the genuine springs of action. For instance, the individual 'has too high an opinion of himself to tolerate the thought of his having acted wrongly, and so offence is called for to deflect attention from his own misstep, and this is achieved by identifying him as the wronged party... Taking satisfaction in being the wronged party, one must invent wrongs to feed this self-indulgence.'[11] The autonomous nature of action is thereby concealed; it is *the other party*, charged with the original misconduct, with the starting-it-all felony, that is cast as the true actor of the drama. The self stays thereby wholly on the receiving side; the self is a *sufferer of the other's action* rather than an actor in its own right.

Once embraced, such a vision seems to be self-propelling and self-reinforcing. To retain credibility, the outrage imputed to the other side must be ever more awesome and above all ever less curable or redeemable; and the resulting sufferings of the victim must be declared ever more abominable and painful, so that the self-declared victim may go on justifying ever harsher measures 'in the just response' to the offence committed or 'in defence' against offences yet to be committed. 'Constrained' actions need constantly *to deny* their autonomy. It is for that reason that they constitute the most radical obstacle to the admission of the self's sovereignty and to the self's acting in a fashion resonant with such an admission.

The overcoming of self-imposed constraints by unmasking and discrediting the self-deception they rest on emerges therefore as the preliminary, indispensable condition for giving free rein to sovereign life's expression; an expression that manifests itself, first and foremost, in trust, compassion and mercy.

For most of human history 'immediacy of presence' overlapped with potential and feasible 'immediacy of action'.

Our ancestors had few if any tools that would enable them to act effectively at a great distance – but they were hardly ever exposed to the sight of an occurrence of human suffering too distant to be reached by the tools in hand. The totality of the moral choices our ancestors confronted could be almost completely enclosed within the narrow space of immediacy, face-to-face meetings and interaction. The choice between good and evil, whenever it was faced, could therefore be inspired, influenced and in principle even controlled by the 'sovereign expression of life'.

Today, though, the silence of the ethical command is deafening as never before. That command prompts and covertly directs 'sovereign expressions of life'; but while those expressions have retained their immediacy, the objects that trigger and attract them have sailed away, far beyond the space of proximity/immediacy. In addition to what we may see in our immediate vicinity with the naked (unassisted) eye, we are now exposed daily to the 'mediated' knowledge of *distant* misery and *distant* cruelty. We all now have tele*vision*; but few of us have access to the means of tele-*action*.

If the misery we were able not only to see but also to mitigate or heal cast us in a situation of moral choice which the 'sovereign expression of life' would be able to handle (even if it was excruciatingly difficult) – the widening gap between what we are (indirectly) made aware of and what we can (directly) influence raises the uncertainty that accompanies all moral choices to unprecedented heights, where our ethical endowment is not accustomed, and perhaps is even unable, to operate.

From that painful, perhaps unbearable realization of impotence, we are tempted to run for shelter. The temptation to render 'the difficult to deal with' into 'the unreachable' is constant, and rising . . .

'The more we detach ourselves from our immediate surroundings, the more we rely on surveillance of that environment . . . Homes in many urban areas around the world now exist to protect their inhabitants, not to integrate people with their communities,' observe Gumpert and Drucker.[12]

'As their residents extend their communication spaces to the international sphere, they often simultaneously turn their homes away from public life through increasingly "smart" security infrastructures,' comment Graham and Marvin.[13] 'Virtually all cities across the world are starting to display spaces and zones that are powerfully connected to other "valued" spaces across the urban landscape as well as across national, international and even global distances. At the same time, though, there is often a palpable and increasing sense of local disconnection in such places from physically close, but socially and economically distant, places and people.'[14]

The waste product of the new extraterritoriality-through-connectedness of the privileged urban spaces, inhabited and used by the global elite, are the disconnected and abandoned spaces – Michael Schwarzer's 'ghost wards', where 'dreams have been replaced by nightmares and danger and violence are more commonplace than elsewhere.'[15] To keep the distances impassable and stave off the dangers of leakage and the contamination of regional purity, handy tools are zero tolerance and exiling the homeless from spaces where they can make a living but where they also make themselves obtrusively and vexingly visible, to off-limits spaces where they can do neither.

As first suggested by Manuel Castells, there is a growing polarization, and an ever more complete break in communication between the lifeworlds of the two categories of city residents:

> The space of the upper tier is usually connected to global communication and to a vast network of exchange, open to messages and experiences that embrace the entire world. At the other end of the spectrum, segmented local networks, often ethnically based, rely on their identity as the most valuable resource to defend their interests, and ultimately their being.[16]

The picture emerging from this description is of two segregated and separate lifeworlds. Only the second of the two is territorially circumscribed and can be grasped in the net of orthodox geographical, mundane and 'down to earth' notions. Those who live in the first of the two distinct lifeworlds may be, like the others, *'in* the place', but they are not *'of* that place' – certainly not spiritually, but also quite often, whenever they wish, not bodily.

The 'upper tier' people do not belong to the place they inhabit since their concerns lie (or rather float) elsewhere. One may guess that apart from being left alone and so free to engross themselves fully in their own pastimes, and being assured of the services needed for life's daily needs and comforts (however defined), they have no other vested interests in the city in which their residences are located. The city population is not, as it used to be for the factory owners and the merchants of consumables and ideas of yore, their grazing ground, source of their wealth or a ward in their custody, care and responsibility. They are therefore, by and large, *unconcerned* with the affairs of 'their' city, just one locality among many, all such localities being small and insignificant from the vantage point of cyberspace – their genuine, even if virtual, home.

The lifeworld of the other, 'lower' tier of city residents is the very opposite of the first. It is defined mostly by being cut off from that worldwide network of communication by which the 'upper tier' people are connected and to which their lives are tuned. The lower-tier city dwellers are 'doomed to stay local' – and so one could and should expect their attention, complete with discontents, dreams and hopes, to focus on 'local affairs'. For them, it is inside the city they inhabit that the battle for survival and a decent place in the world is launched, waged, sometimes won but mostly lost.

The secession of the new global elite from its past engagements with the local *populus* and the widening gap between the living/ lived spaces of those who seceded and those who have been left behind is arguably the most seminal of social, cultural and political departures associated with the passage from the 'solid' to the 'liquid' stage of modernity.

There is a lot of truth, and nothing but the truth, in the picture sketched above. But not the whole truth.

The most significant part of the truth that is missing or played down is the part that more than any of the others accounts for the most vital (and probably, in the long run, the most consequential) characteristic of contemporary urban life. The characteristic in question is the intimate interplay between globalizing pressures and the fashion in which identities of place are negotiated, formed and reformed.

It is a grave mistake to locate the 'global' and the 'local' aspects of contemporary living conditions and life politics in two different spaces that only marginally and occasionally communicate, as the opting out of the 'upper tier' would ultimately suggest. In his recently published study, Michael Peter Smith objects to the view (as suggested, in his opinion, by David Harvey or John Friedman among others) that opposes 'a dynamic but placeless logic of global economic flows' to 'a static image of place and local culture', now 'valorized' as the 'life place' 'of being-in-the-world'.[17] In Smith's own opinion, 'far from reflecting a static ontology of "being" or "community", localities are dynamic constructions "in the making".'

Indeed, the line separating the abstract, 'somewhere in the nowhere' space of global operators from the fleshy, tangible, supremely 'here and now' space-within-reach of the 'locals' can be easily drawn only in the ethereal world of theory, in which the tangled and intertwined contents of human lifeworlds are first 'straightened up' and then filed and boxed, for the sake of clarity, each in its own compartment. The realities of city life, though, play havoc with such neat divisions. Elegant models of urban life and the sharp oppositions deployed in their construction may give a lot of intellectual satisfaction to the theory-builders, but little practical guidance to the urban planners, and even less support to the urban dwellers struggling with the challenges of city living.

The real powers that shape the conditions under which we all act these days flow in global space, while our institutions of political action remain by and large tied to the ground; they are, as before, local.

Because they stay mainly local, political agencies operating in urban space tend to be fatally afflicted with an insufficiency of the power to act, and particularly to act effectively and in a sovereign manner, on the stage where the drama of politics is played. Another result, though, is the dearth of politics in extraterritorial cyberspace, the playground of powers.

In our globalizing world, politics tends to be increasingly, passionately, self-consciously *local*. Evicted from, or barred access to cyberspace, politics falls back and rebounds on affairs that are 'within reach', on local matters and neighbourhood relations. For most of us and for most of the time, these seem to be *the only* issues we can 'do something about', influence, repair, improve, redirect. Only in local matters can our action or inaction 'make a difference', whereas for other, admittedly 'supralocal' affairs there is (or so we are repeatedly told by our political leaders and all other 'people in the know') 'no alternative'. We come to suspect that, given the pitifully inadequate means and resources at our disposal, things will take their course whatever we do or whatever we could sensibly contemplate doing.

Even matters with undoubtedly global, far-away and recondite sources and causes enter the realm of political concerns solely through their local offshoots and repercussions. The global pollution of air or water supplies turns into a *political* matter when a dumping ground for toxic waste is allocated next door, in 'our own backyard', in frighteningly close, but also encouragingly 'within

100

reach' proximity to our homeground. The progressive commercialization of health concerns, obviously an effect of the unbridled chase for profit by supranational pharmaceutical giants, comes into political view when the hospital serving a neighbourhood is run down or the local old people's homes and mental care institutions are phased out. It was the residents of one city, New York, who had to cope with the havoc caused by globally gestated terrorism, and the councils and mayors of other cities who had to assume responsibility for the protection of individual safety now seen as vulnerable to forces entrenched far beyond the reach of any municipality. The global devastation of livelihoods and the uprooting of long settled populations enter the horizon of political action through the colourful 'economic migrants' crowding the streets that once looked so uniformly...

To cut a long story short: *cities have become dumping grounds for globally begotten problems.* The residents of cities and their elected representatives tend to be confronted with a task they can by no stretch of imagination fulfil: the task of finding local solutions to global contradictions.

Hence the paradox noted by Castells, of 'increasingly local politics in a world structured by increasingly global processes'. 'There was production of meaning and identity: my neighbourhood, my community, my city, my school, my tree, my river, my beach, my chapel, my peace, my environment.' 'Defenceless against the global whirlwind, people stuck to themselves.'[18] Let us note that the more 'stuck to themselves' they are, the more defenceless they tend to become 'against the global whirlwind', and also the more helpless in deciding the local, and so ostensibly their own, meanings and identities – to the great joy of global operators, who have no reason to fear the defenceless.

As Castells implies elsewhere, the creation of the 'space of flows' sets a new (global) hierarchy of domination-through-the-threat-of-disengagement. The 'space of flows' can 'escape the control of any locale' – while (and because!) 'the space of places is fragmented, localized, and thus increasingly powerless vis-à-vis the versatility of the space of flows, with the only chance of resistance for localities being to refuse landing rights for overwhelming flows

– only to see that they land in the locale nearby, inducing there-fore the bypassing and marginalization of rebellious commu-nities.'[19]

Local politics – and particularly urban politics – has become hopelessly overloaded – much beyond its carrying/performing cap-acity. It is now expected to mitigate the consequences of out-of-control globalization with means and resources that self-same globalization rendered pitifully inadequate.

No one in our fast globalizing world is a 'global operator' pure and simple. The most that the members of the globally influential and globetrotting elite can manage is a wider scope for their mobility.

If things get too hot for comfort and the space around their city residences proves too hazardous and too difficult to manage, they may move elsewhere; they have an option not available to the rest of their (physically) close neighbours. Such an option to escape local discomforts gives them an independence of which other urban residents can only dream, and the luxury of a lofty indiffer-ence that those others cannot afford. Their commitment to 'put-ting the city's affairs in order' tends to be considerably less complete and unconditional than the commitment of those who have less freedom to break local bonds unilaterally.

This does not mean, however, that in their search for 'meaning and identity', which they need and crave no less intensely than the next person, the globally connected elite can leave out of account the place in which they live and work. Like all other men and women, they are part of the cityscape, and their life pursuits, willy-nilly, are inscribed in it. As global operators, they may roam cyberspace. But as human agents, they are, day in day out, con-fined to the physical space in which they operate, to the environ-ment preset and continually reprocessed in the course of human struggles for meaning and identity. Human experience is formed and gleaned, life-sharing managed, its meaning conceived, absorbed and negotiated, around *places*. And it is *in places* and *of places* that human urges and desires are gestated and incubated, live in hope of fulfilment, risk frustration and are indeed, more often than not, frustrated.

Contemporary cities are the battlegrounds on which global powers and stubbornly local meanings and identities meet, clash, struggle and seek a satisfactory, or just bearable, settlement – a mode of cohabitation that is hoped to be a lasting peace but as a rule proves to be but an armistice, an interval to repair broken defences and redeploy fighting units. It is that confrontation, and not any single factor, that sets in motion and guides the dynamics of the 'liquid modern' city.

And let there be no mistake: *any* city, even if not all to the same degree. Michael Peter Smith on his recent trip to Copenhagen has recorded walking in a single hour 'past small groups of Turkish, African, and Middle Eastern immigrants', observing 'several veiled and unveiled Arab women', reading 'signs in various non-European languages', and having 'an interesting conversation with an Irish bartender, in an English pub, across from Tivoli Garden'.[20] These field experiences proved to be helpful, says Smith, in the talk on transnational connections he gave in Copenhagen later in the week, 'when a questioner insisted that transnationalism was a phenomenon that might apply to "global cities" like New York or London, but had little relevance to more insular places like Copenhagen'.

The recent history of American cities is full of U-turns – but it is marked all over with security and safety concerns.

What we learn, for instance, from John Hannigan's study[21] is that a sudden horror of crime lurking in the dark corners of the inner city struck the inhabitants of American metropolitan areas in the second half of the last century and led to a 'white flight' from the city centres – though only a few years before those 'inner cities' had become powerful magnets for crowds eager to revel in the kinds of mass entertainment that only the centres of big cities – and not other, less densely populated urban areas – could offer.

No matter whether that dread of crime was well grounded or whether the sudden upsurge of criminality was a figment of feverish imaginations, deserted and abandoned inner cities, a 'dwindling number of pleasure seekers and an ever greater perception of cities as dangerous places to be', were the result. Of one of such cities, Detroit, another author noted in 1989 that its 'streets are so deserted after dusk that the city appears to be a ghost town – like Washington, DC; the nation's capital'.[22]

Hannigan found out that a reverse trend had started towards the end of the century. After many lean years of 'don't go out tonight' panic and the 'desertification' it brought to cities, American town elders combined with promoters in a struggle to make town centres fun again, an irresistible attraction for would-be revellers, as 'entertainment returns to the city centre' and 'out-of-town day-trippers' are drawn back to the inner city in the hope of finding there something 'exciting, safe and not available in the suburbs'.[23]

Admittedly, such sharp, neurotic U-turns in the plight of cities in the United States, with their long festering, usually seething and occasionally erupting race antagonisms and enmities, may be more salient and abrupt than elsewhere, where race conflict and prejudice add less or no fuel to the smouldering sentiments of uncertainty and confusion. In a somewhat lighter, more attenuated form, the ambivalence of attraction and repulsion and the alternation of passion for and aversion to big city life mark, however, the most recent history of many, perhaps the majority of, European cities.

City and social change are almost synonymous. Change is the quality of city life and the mode of urban existence. Change and city may, and indeed should, be defined by reference to each other. Why is it so, though? Why must this be so?

It is common to define the cities as places where strangers meet, remain in each other's proximity and interact for a long time without ceasing to be strangers to each other. Focusing on the role cities play in economic development, Jane Jacobs points to the sheer density of human communication as the prime cause of that characteristically urban restlessness.[24] City dwellers are not necessarily smarter than other human beings – but the density of space occupation results in a concentration of needs. And so questions are asked in the city that have not been asked elsewhere, problems arise which people have had no occasion to cope with under different conditions. Facing problems and asking questions present a challenge, and stretch the inventiveness of humans to unprecedented lengths. This in turn offers a tempting chance to other people who live in more relaxed, but also less promising places: city life constantly attracts newcomers, and the trademark of newcomers is to bring 'new ways of looking at things, and maybe new ways of solving old problems'. Newcomers are strangers to the city, and things that the old, well-settled residents stopped noticing because of their familiarity seem bizarre and to call for an explanation when seen through the eyes of a stranger. For the strangers, and particularly for the newcomers among them, nothing in the city is 'natural', they take nothing for granted. Newcomers are born and sworn enemies of tranquillity and self-congratulation.

This is not perhaps a situation to be enjoyed by the city's natives – but it is also their good luck. The city is at its best, most exuberant and most lavish in the opportunities it offers when its ways and means are challenged, questioned and put on the defendant's bench. Michael Storper, economist, geographer and planner,[25] ascribes the intrinsic buoyancy and creativity typical of dense urban living to the uncertainty that arises from the poorly coordinated and forever a-changing relationship 'between the parts of complex organizations, between individuals, and between individuals and organizations' – unavoidable under the city's conditions of high density and close proximity.

Strangers are not a modern invention – but strangers who remain strangers for a long time to come, even in perpetuity, are. In a typical premodern town or village strangers were not allowed to stay strange for long. Some of them were chased away, or not let in through the city gates in the first place. Those who wished and were permitted to enter and stay longer tended to be 'familiarized' – closely questioned and quickly 'domesticated' – so that they could join the network of relationships like established city dwellers: in *personal* mode. This had its consequences – strikingly different from the processes familiar to us from the experience of contemporary, modern, crowded and densely populated cities.

Whatever happens to cities in their history, and however drastically their spatial structure, look and style may change over the years or centuries, one feature remains constant: cities are spaces where strangers stay and move in close proximity to each other.

Being a permanent component of city life, the perpetual and ubiquitous presence of strangers within sight and reach adds a good measure of perpetual uncertainty to the life pursuits of all city dwellers. That presence, impossible to avoid for more than a brief moment, is a source of anxiety that never dries up, and of an aggressiveness that is usually dormant, yet time and again is liable to erupt.

The ambient, even if subliminal, fear of the unknown desperately seeks credible outlets. Accumulated anxieties tend to be unloaded against the selected category of 'aliens', picked up to epitomize the 'strangeness', the unfamiliarity, the opacity of the life setting, the vagueness of the risk and threat as such. When a selected category of 'aliens' is chased away from homes and shops, the frightening ghost of uncertainty is, for a time, exorcized; the horrifying monster of insecurity is burnt in effigy. Border barriers painstakingly erected against 'false asylum seekers' and 'merely economic' migrants carry the hope of fortifying a shaky, erratic and unpredictable existence. But liquid modern life is bound to stay erratic and capricious whatever plight is visited on 'undesirable aliens', and so the relief is short-lived, and the hopes attached to the 'tough and decisive measures' are dashed as soon as they are raised.

The stranger is, by definition, an agent moved by intentions that one can at best guess but would never know for sure. The stranger is the unknown variable in all equations calculated when decisions about what to do and how to behave are pondered; and so even if the strangers do not become objects of overt aggression and are not openly and actively resented, the presence of strangers inside the field of action remains discomforting, as it makes a tall order of the task of predicting the effects of action and its chances of success or failure.

Sharing space with strangers, living in the uninvited yet obtrusive proximity of strangers, is a condition that city residents find difficult, perhaps impossible to escape. The proximity of strangers is their fate, and a *modus vivendi* must be experimented with, tried and tested, and (hopefully) found to make cohabitation palatable and life livable. This need is 'given', non-negotiable; but the way in which city residents go about satisfying this need is a matter of choice. And that choice is made daily – whether by commission or by omission, by design or default.

Of São Paulo, the second largest Brazilian city, bustling and fast expanding, Teresa Caldeira writes: 'São Paulo is today a city of walls. Physical barriers have been constructed everywhere – around houses, apartment buildings, parks, squares, office complexes and schools... A new aesthetics of security shapes all types of constructions and imposes a new logic of surveillance and distance...'[26]

Those who can afford it buy themselves a residence in a 'condominium', intended as a hermitage: physically inside, but socially and spiritually outside the city. 'Closed communities are supposed to be separate worlds. Their advertisements propose a "total way of life" which would represent an alternative to the quality of life offered by the city and its deteriorated public space.' A most prominent feature of the condominium is its 'isolation and distance from the city... Isolation means separation from those considered to be socially inferior' and as the developers and the real-estate agents insist, 'the key factor to assure this is security. This means fences and walls surrounding the condominium, guards on duty twenty-four hours a day controlling the entrances, and an array of facilities and services' 'for keeping the others out'.

As we all know, fences have to have two sides. Fences divide otherwise uniform space into an 'inside' and an 'outside', but what is 'inside' for those on one side of the fence is 'outside' for those on the other. The residents of condominiums fence themselves 'out' of the off-putting, discomfiting, vaguely threatening, rough life of the city – and 'in' the oasis of calm and safety. By the same token, though, they fence all the others out of the decent and secure places whose standards they are prepared and determined to keep up and defend tooth and nail, and into the self-same shabby and squalid streets which they try, no expense spared, to fence off. The fence separates the 'voluntary ghetto' of the high and mighty from the many enforced ones of the down and out. For the insiders of the voluntary ghetto, the other ghettos are spaces 'we won't go in'. For the insiders of the involuntary ghettos, the area to which they are confined (by being excluded from elsewhere) is the space 'we are not allowed to get out of'.

In São Paulo the segregationist and exclusionist tendency shows itself at its most brutal, unscrupulous and unashamed; but its impact can be found, albeit in a somewhat attenuated form, in most metropolitan cities.

Paradoxically, the cities originally constructed to provide safety for all their inhabitants are these days associated more often with danger than with security. As Nan Elin puts it, 'the fear factor [in the construction and reconstruction of cities] has certainly grown, as indicated by the growth in locked car and house doors and security systems, the popularity of "gated" and "secure" communities for all age and income groups, and the increasing surveillance of public spaces, not to mention the unending reports of danger emitted by the mass media.'[27]

Genuine and putative threats to the body and the property of the individual are fast turning into major considerations whenever the merits or disadvantages of a place to live are contemplated. They have also been assigned the top position in real-estate marketing policy. Uncertainty for the future, frailty of social position and existential insecurity, those ubiquitous accompaniments of life in a 'liquid modern' world rooted notoriously in remote places and so removed from individual control, tend to be focused on the nearest targets and channelled into concerns with personal safety; the kinds of concerns that are condensed in turn into segregationist/exclusionist urges, inexorably leading to urban space wars.

As we can learn from the perceptive study of the young American architectural/urbanist critic Steven Flusty,[28] servicing that war, and particularly the designing of ways to bar adversaries, current, potential and putative, from access to the claimed space and to keep them at a safe distance from it, constitutes the most widely and rapidly expanding concern of architectural innovation and urban development in American cities. The novel, most proudly advertised and widely imitated constructions are 'interdictory spaces' – 'designed to intercept, repel or filter the would-be users'. Explicitly, the purpose of 'interdictory spaces' is to divide, segregate and exclude – not to build bridges, easy passages and meeting places, facilitate communication and otherwise bring the city's residents together.

The architectural/urbanist inventions distinguished, listed and named by Flusty are the technically updated equivalents of pre-modern moats, turrets and embrasures of city walls; but rather than defending the city and all its dwellers against the enemy outside, they are erected to set and keep the city's residents apart and to defend them against each other, now cast in the status of adversaries. Among the inventions named by Flusty there is 'slippery space' – 'space that cannot be reached, due to contorted, protracted, or missing paths of approach'; 'prickly space' – 'space that cannot be comfortably occupied, defended by such details as wall-mounted sprinkler heads activated to clear loiterers or ledges sloped to inhibit sitting'; and 'jittery space' – 'space that cannot be utilized unobserved due to active monitoring by roving patrols and/or remote technologies feeding to security stations'. These and other kinds of 'interdictory spaces' have but one, though composite, purpose: to cut extraterritorial enclaves out of the continuous city territory, to erect little fortresses inside which the members of the supraterritorial global elite may groom, cultivate and relish their bodily independence and spiritual isolation from locality. In the landscape of the city 'interdictory spaces' become landmarks of the *disintegration* of locally grounded, shared communal living.

The developments described by Steven Flusty are high-tech manifestations of the ubiquitous *mixophobia*.

Mixophobia is a highly predictable and widespread reaction to the mind-boggling, spine-chilling and nerve-breaking variety of human types and lifestyles that rub shoulders in the streets of contemporary cities and in the most 'ordinary' (read: unprotected by 'interdictory spaces') of their living districts. As the polyvocality and cultural variegation of the urban environment in the global-ization era sets in – with the likelihood that it will intensify rather than be mitigated over the course of time – the tensions arising from the vexing/confusing/irritating unfamiliarity of the setting will probably go on prompting segregationist urges.

Expressing such urges may (temporarily, yet repeatedly) relieve rising tensions. It offers hope: off-putting and disconcerting differ-ences might be unassailable and intractable, but perhaps the poison may be drawn out of the sting by assigning to each form of life its separate, inclusive as well as exclusive, well-marked and well-guarded physical space. Short of that radical solution, per-haps one could at least secure for oneself, for one's kith and kin and other 'people like oneself' a territory free from that jumble and mess that irredeemably afflicts other city areas. Mixophobia mani-fests itself in the drive towards islands of similarity and sameness amidst the sea of variety and difference.

The roots of mixophobia are banal – not at all difficult to locate, easy to understand if not necessarily easy to forgive. As Richard Sennett suggests, 'the "we" feeling, which expresses a desire to be similar, is a way for men to avoid the necessity of looking deeper into each other.' It promises, we may say, some spiritual comfort: the prospect of making togetherness easier to bear by cutting off the effort to understand, to negotiate, to compromise, that living amidst and with difference requires. 'Innate to the process of forming a coherent image of community is the desire to avoid actual participation. Feeling common bonds without common experience occurs in the first place because men are afraid of participation, afraid of the dangers and the challenges of it, afraid of its pain.'[29]

The drive towards a 'community of similarity' is a sign of withdrawal not just from the otherness outside, but also from commitment to the lively yet turbulent, invigorating yet cumber-some interaction inside. The attraction of a 'community of same-ness' is that of an insurance policy against the risks with which daily life in a polyvocal world is fraught. It does not decrease, let alone stave off the risks. Like all palliatives, it only promises a shelter from some of their most immediate and most feared effects.

Choosing the escape option prompted by mixophobia has an insidious and deleterious consequence of its own: the strategy is increasingly self-perpetuating and self-reinforcing the more ineffective it is. Sennett explains why this is – indeed, must be – the case: 'Cities in America during the past two decades have grown in such a way that ethnic areas become relatively homogeneous; it appears no accident that the fear of the outsider has also grown to the extent that these ethnic communities have been cut off.'[30] The longer people stay in a uniform environment – in the company of others 'like themselves' with whom they can 'socialize' perfunctorily and matter-of-factly without incurring the risk of miscomprehension and without struggling with the vexing need to translate between distinct universes of meaning – the more they are likely to 'delearn' the art of negotiating shared meanings and a *modus covivendi*.

Since they have forgotten or neglected to acquire the skills necessary for living with difference, it is little wonder that such people view the prospect of confronting strangers face-to-face with rising horror. Strangers tend to appear ever more frightening as they become increasingly alien, unfamiliar and incomprehensible, and as the dialogue and interaction which could eventually assimilate their 'otherness' to one's own lifeworld fade, or never take off in the first place. The drive to a homogeneous, territorially isolated environment may be triggered by mixophobia; but *practising* territorial separation is life-belt and food purveyor to that same mixophobia.

Mixophobia, though, is not the sole combatant on the urban battlefield.

City living is a notoriously ambivalent experience. It attracts *and* repels, but to make the plight of the city dweller more complex yet, it is *the same* aspects of city life that, intermittently or simultaneously, attract and repel... The confusing variety of the urban environment is a source of fear (particularly for those people among us who have already 'lost the familiar ways', having been cast into a state of acute uncertainty by the destabilizing processes of globalization). The same kaleidoscope-like twinkle and glimmer of urban scenery, never short of novelty and surprise, constitute however its difficult-to-resist charm and seductive power.

Confronting the never-ending and constantly dazzling spectacle of the city is therefore not experienced unambiguously as a bane and a curse; nor does taking shelter from it feel like an unmixed blessing. The city prompts *mixophilia* as much as, and simultaneously with, mixophobia. City life is an intrinsically and irreparably *ambivalent* affair.

The bigger and more heterogeneous a city, the more attractions it may support and offer. The massive condensation of strangers is simultaneously a repellent and a most powerful magnet, drawing to the city ever new cohorts of men and women weary of the monotony of rural or small-town life, fed up with its repetitive routine – and despairing of its prospectless dearth of chances. Variety is a promise of opportunities, many and different opportunities, opportunities fitting all skills and any taste – and so the bigger the city the more likely it is to attract a growing number of people who reject or are refused accommodation and life chances in places that are smaller and so less tolerant of idiosyncrasy and more tight-fisted in the opportunities they offer. It seems that mixophilia, just like mixophobia, is a self-propelling, self-propagating and self-invigorating tendency. Neither of the two is likely to exhaust itself, nor lose any of its vigour in the course of city renewal and the refurbishment of city space.

Mixophobia and mixophilia coexist in every city, but they coexist as well inside every one of the city's residents. Admittedly, this is an uneasy coexistence, full of sound and fury – though signifying a lot to people on the receiving end of liquid modern ambivalence.

Since strangers are bound to carry on their lives in each other's company whatever the future twists and turns of urban history, the art of living peacefully and happily with difference and of benefiting, undisturbed, from the variety of stimuli and opportunities acquires paramount importance among the skills a city resident has to learn and display.

Even if, given the rising human mobility of the liquid modern epoch and the accelerated change in the cast, plots and settings of the urban scene, the complete eradication of mixophobia is not on the cards – perhaps something can be done to influence the proportions in which mixophilia and mixophobia are combined and so to reduce the confusing, anxiety-and-anguish-generating impact of mixophobia. Indeed, it seems that architects and urban planners could do quite a lot to assist the growth of mixophilia and minimize the occasions for mixophobic responses to the challenges of city life. And there seems to be a lot that they might do and indeed are doing to facilitate the opposite effects.

As we have seen before, the segregation of residential areas and publicly attended spaces, commercially attractive to developers and attractive to their clients as a fast fix for mixophobia-generated anxieties, is in fact mixophobia's prime cause. The solutions on offer create, so to speak, the problems they claim to resolve: builders of gated communities and closely guarded condominiums and architects of 'interdictory spaces' create, reproduce and intensify the need and the demand they claim to satisfy.

Mixophobic paranoia feeds upon itself and acts as a self-fulfilling prophecy. If segregation is offered and taken up as a radical cure for the danger represented by strangers, cohabitation with strangers becomes more difficult by the day. Homogenizing living quarters and then reducing to an unavoidable minimum all commerce and communication between them is a foolproof recipe for making the urge to exclude and segregate more intense and deeper. Such a measure may help to reduce the pains suffered by people afflicted with mixophobia, but the cure is itself pathogenic and deepens the affliction, so that ever new and stronger doses of the medicine are needed to keep the pain at a tolerably low level. Social homogeneity of space, emphasized and fortified by spatial segregation, lowers in its residents their tolerance to difference and so multiplies the occasions for mixophobic reactions, making city life look more 'risk-prone' and so more agonizing, rather than making it feel more secure and so easier-going and more enjoyable.

More favourable to the entrenchment and cultivation of mixophiliac sentiments would be the opposite strategy by architects and urban planners: the propagation of open, inviting and hospitable public spaces which all categories of urban residents would be tempted to attend regularly and knowingly and willingly share.

As Hans Gadamer famously pointed out in his *Truth and Method*, mutual understanding is prompted by the 'fusion of horizons' – cognitive horizons, that is, horizons that are drawn and expanded in the course of the accumulation of life experience. The 'fusion' that mutual understanding requires may only be the outcome of *shared* experience; and sharing experience is inconceivable without shared space.

As if to supply massive empirical proof of Gadamer's hypothesis, it has been found that spaces reserved for face-to-face meetings – or just sharing space, 'mixing with', 'being around' together, like dining in the same restaurants or drinking in the same bars – of travelling business people and other members of the emergent globetrotting elite or 'global ruling class' (places like the global chains of supranational hotels and conference centres) play a crucial role in the integration of that elite despite the cultural, linguistic, denominational, ideological or any other differences that would otherwise split it and prevent the development of the sentiment that 'we belong together'.[31]

Indeed, the development of mutual understanding and the sharing of life experiences that such understanding needs is the sole reason why, despite having the facility to communicate faster electronically and with much less hassle and drudgery, business people and academics go on travelling and visiting each other and meeting at conferences. If communication could be reduced to the transfer of information and no 'fusion of horizons' was called for, then in our age of the internet and the worldwide web, physical contact and the (even if temporary and intermittent) sharing of space and experience would have become redundant. But it has not, and nothing suggests thus far that it will.

There are things that the architects and city planners may do to shift the balance between mixophobia and mixophilia in favour of the latter (just as they, by commission or omission, contribute to the opposite drift). But there are limits to what they can achieve while acting alone and relying solely on the effects of their own actions.

The roots of mixophobia – the allergic, febrile sensitivity to strangers and the strange – lie beyond the reach of architectural competence or the city planner's remit. These roots are sunk deep in the existential condition of contemporary men and women born and bred in the deregulated, individualized, fluid world of accelerated and diffuse change. However important for the quality of daily life may be the shape, the look, the atmosphere of the city's streets and the uses to which city spaces are put, they are but some and not necessarily the paramount factors contributing to that destabilizing condition breeding uncertainty and anxiety.

More than anything else, mixophobic sentiments are prompted and fed by an overwhelming feeling of insecurity. It is insecure men and women, uncertain of their place in the world, of their life prospects and the effects of their own actions, who are most vulnerable to the temptation of mixophobia and most likely to fall into its trap. The trap consists in channelling the anxiety away from its true roots and unloading it on targets unrelated to its sources. As a result, many human beings are victimized (and in the long run the victimizers invite victimization in their turn) while the sources of the anguish stay protected from interference and emerge from the operation unscathed and intact.

What follows is that the troubles that afflict contemporary cities cannot be resolved by reforming the city itself, however radical such a reform may be. There are, let me repeat, *no local solutions to globally generated problems*. The kind of 'security' that the urban developers offer is impotent to relieve, let alone to eradicate, the existential insecurity replenished daily by the fluidity of labour markets, by the fragility of the value ascribed to past or currently pursued skills and competences, by the acknowledged vulnerability of human bonds and the assumed precariousness and revocability of commitments and partnerships. A reform of the existential condition needs to precede reforms of the city since it conditions their success. Without that reform, efforts confined to the city to overcome or detoxify mixophobic pressures are bound to remain just palliatives; more often than not, just placebos.

This needs to be remembered, not in order to devalue or play down the difference between good and bad architecture or proper and improper city planning (both may be and often are enormously important for the quality of life of city residents), but to set the task in a perspective that includes all the factors that are decisive in making the right choice and making that right choice stick.

Contemporary cities are dumping grounds for the misformed and deformed products of fluid modern society (while, to be sure, themselves contributing to the accumulation of waste).

There are no solutions centred on the city, let alone confined to the city, to meet systemic contradictions and malfunctions – and however enormous and laudable the imagination of the architects, city mayors and municipal counsellors may be, they won't be found. Problems need to be met where they arise: the troubles confronted and suffered inside the city sprouted up elsewhere and the expanses where they incubate and gestate are too vast to be tackled with the tools made to the size of even the largest conurbation. Those expanses extend even beyond the reach of the sovereign action of the nation-state, the largest, most commodious and inclusive setting for democratic procedures invented and put in place in modern times. Those expanses are *global*, and increasingly so; and so far we have not come anywhere near inventing, let alone deploying, means of democratic control that match the size and the potency of the forces to be controlled.

This is, without doubt, a long-term task and a task that will require more, much more thought, action and endurance than any reform of urban planning and architectural aesthetics. This does not mean, though, that efforts towards such reforms need to be suspended until we grapple with the roots of the trouble and bring under control those dangerously loose globalizing trends. If anything, the contrary is true – since whereas the city is the dumping ground for anxieties and apprehensions generated by globally induced uncertainty and insecurity, it is also a prime training ground where the means to placate and disperse that uncertainty and insecurity can be experimented with, tried out and eventually learned and adopted.

It is in the city that the strangers who confront each other in global space as hostile states, inimical civilizations or military adversaries meet as *individual human beings*, watch each other at close quarters, talk to each other, learn each other's ways, negotiate the rules of life in common, cooperate and sooner or later get used to each other's presence and on an increasing number of occasions find pleasure in sharing each other's company. After such admittedly local training those strangers may be much less tense and apprehensive when it comes to handling global affairs: incompatible civilizations may seem to be not that incompatible after all, mutual hostility not as intractable as it appeared and sabre-rattling not the sole way of resolving mutual conflicts. Gadamer's 'fusion of horizons' may become a somewhat more realistic project if pursued (even if by trial and error and with but mixed success) in city streets.

Coming to terms with the new global situation, and particularly confronting it effectively, will take time – just as all truly profound, watershed-like transformations of the human condition have always done.
As in the case of all such transformations, it is impossible (and highly inadvisable to try) to pre-empt history and to predict, let alone predesign, the form it will take and the settlement to which it will eventually lead. But such a confrontation will have to take place. It will probably constitute a major preoccupation and fill most of the history of the century just starting.

The drama will be staged and plotted in both spaces – on both the global and the local scenes. The dénouements of the two stage

117

productions are closely intertwined and depend intimately on how deeply the scriptwriters and the actors in each production are aware of that link and with how much skill and determination they contribute to the other production's success.

Togetherness Dismantled

A spectre hovers over the planet: the spectre of xenophobia. Old and new, never extinguished and freshly defrosted and warmed up tribal suspicions and animosities have mixed and blended with the brand-new fear for safety distilled from the uncertainties and insecurities of liquid modern existence.

People worn out and dead tired as a result of forever inconclusive tests of adequacy, and frightened to the raw by the mysterious, inexplicable precariousness of their fortunes and by the global mists hiding their prospects from view, desperately seek culprits for their trials and tribulations. They find them, unsurprisingly, under the nearest lamp-post – in the only spot obligingly illuminated by the forces of law and order: 'It is the criminals who make us insecure, and it is the outsiders who cause crime'; and so 'it is rounding up, incarcerating and deporting the outsiders that will restore our lost or stolen security.'

To his summary of the most recent shifts in the European political spectrum Donald G. McNeil Jr gave the title 'Politicians pander to fear of crime'.[1] Indeed, throughout the world ruled by democratically elected governments the sentence 'I'll be tough on crime' has turned out to be the trump card that beats all others, but the winning hand is almost invariably a combination of a promise of 'more prisons, more policemen, longer sentences' with an oath of 'no immigration, no asylum rights, no naturalization'. As

McNeil put it, 'Politicians across Europe use the "outsiders cause crime" stereotype to link ethnic hatred, which is unfashionable, to the more palatable fear for one's own safety.'

The Chirac versus Jospin duel for the French presidency in 2002 was only in its preliminary stages when it degenerated into a public auction in which both competitors vied for electoral support by offering ever harsher measures against criminals and immigrants, but above all against the immigrants that breed crime and the criminality bred by immigrants.[2] First of all, though, they did their best to refocus the anxiety of electors that stemmed from the ambient sense of *precarité* (an infuriating insecurity of social position intertwined with an acute uncertainty about the future of the means of livelihood) onto a fear for personal safety (integrity of the body, personal possessions, home and neighbourhood). On 14 July 2001 Chirac set the infernal machine in motion, announcing the need to fight 'that growing threat to safety, that rising flood' in view of an almost 10 per cent increase in delinquency in the first half of the year (also announced on that occasion), and declaring that the 'zero tolerance' policy was bound to become law once he was re-elected. The tune of the presidential campaign had been set, and Jospin was quick to join in, elaborating his own variations on the shared motif (though, unexpectedly for the main soloists, but certainly not for sociologically wise observers, it was Le Pen's voice that came out on top as the purest and so the most audible).

On 28 August Jospin proclaimed 'the battle against insecurity', vowing 'no laxity', while on 6 September Daniel Vaillant and Marylise Lebranchu, his ministers of, respectively, internal affairs and justice, swore that they would show no tolerance to delin-quency in any form. Vaillant's immediate reaction to the events of 11 September in America was to increase the powers of the police aimed principally against the juveniles of the 'ethnically alien' *banlieues*, the vast housing estates on the outshirts of cities, where according to the official (convenient to officials) version the devilish concoction of uncertainty and insecurity, poisoning the lives of Frenchmen, was brewed. Jospin himself went on castigating and reviling, in ever more vitriolic terms, the 'angelic school' of the softly-softly approach, swearing he had

120

never belonged to it in the past and would never join it in the future. The auction went on, and the bids climbed skywards. Chirac promised to create a ministry of internal security, to which Jospin responded with a commitment to a ministry 'charged with public security' and the 'coordination of police operations'. When Chirac brandished the idea of locked centres for confining juvenile delinquents, Jospin echoed the promise with a vision of 'locked structures' for juvenile offenders, outbidding his opponent with the prospect of 'sentencing on the spot'.

A mere three decades ago Portugal was (alongside Turkey) the main supplier of the 'guest-workers' that the German *Bürger* feared would despoil their homely townscapes and undercut the social compact, the foundation of their security and comfort. Today, thanks to its sharply improved fortunes, Portugal has turned from a labour-exporting into a labour-importing country. The hardships and humiliations suffered when bread had to be earned in foreign countries have been promptly forgotten: 27 per cent of Portuguese have declared that neighbourhoods infested with crime-and-foreigners are their main worry, and the newcomer politician Paulo Portas, playing a single, fiercely anti-immigration card, helped the new right-wing coalition into power (just as happened with Pia Kiersgaard's Danish People's Party in Denmark, Umberto Bossi's Northern League in Italy, and the radically anti-immigrant Progress Party in Norway; all in countries that not so very long ago sent their children to far-away lands to seek the bread which their homelands were too poor to offer).

News like this easily makes front page headlines (like 'UK plan for asylum crackdown' in The *Guardian* of 13 June 2002; no need to mention the headline banners of the tabloids...). The main bulk of immigrant-phobia, however, stays hidden from Western Europe's attention (indeed, knowledge) and never makes it to the surface. 'Blaming the immigrants' – the strangers, the newcomers, and particularly the newcomers among the strangers – for all aspects of social malaise (and first of all for the nauseating, dis-empowering feeling of *Unsicherheit, incertezza, precarité*, in-security) is fast becoming a global habit. As Heather Grabbe, research director of the Centre for European Reform, put it, 'the

Germans blame the Poles, the Poles blame the Ukrainians, the Ukrainians blame the Kirghiz and Uzbeks',[3] while countries too poor to attract any desperately-seeking-a-livelihood neighbours, like Romania, Bulgaria, Hungary or Slovakia, turn their wrath against the usual suspects and stand-by culprits: local but drifting, shunning fixed addresses, and therefore always and everywhere 'newcomers' and outsiders – the Gypsies.

When it comes to the setting of global trends, the US has undisputed priority rights and most of the time holds the initiative. But joining the global trend of immigrant bashing presents America with a rather difficult problem. The US is an admittedly immigrant country: immigration has gone down in American history as a noble pastime, a mission, a heroic exploit of the daring, valiant and brave; so denigration of immigrants, and throwing suspicion on the immigrant's noble calling, would go against the grain of the American identity and perhaps deliver a mortal blow to the American Dream, its undisputed foundation and cement. But efforts are made, by trial and error, to square the circle . . .

On 10 June 2002 high-ranking US officials (FBI Director Robert Mueller, US Deputy Attorney General Larry Thompson, Deputy Defense Secretary Paul Wolfowitz, among others) announced the arrest of a suspected Al-Qaeda terrorist on his return to Chicago from a training trip to Pakistan.[4] As the official version of the affair claimed, an American citizen, American born and bred, Jose Padilla (the name suggests Hispanic roots, that is connected to the latest, relatively poorly settled, addition in a long list of immigrant ethnic affiliations) converted to Islam, took the name of Abdullah al-Mujahir, and promptly went to his new Muslim brethren for instruction in how to harm his erstwhile homeland. He was instructed in the artless art of patching together 'dirty bombs' – 'frighteningly easy to assemble' out of a few ounces of widely available conventional explosives and 'virtually any type of radioactive material' that the would-be terrorists 'can get their hands on' (it was not clear why sophisticated training was needed to assemble weapons 'frighteningly easy to assemble', but when it comes to sowing the seeds of fear for the grapes of wrath to grow, logic is neither here nor there). 'A new phrase entered the post-

Sept. 11 vocabulary of many average Americans: dirty bomb,'
announced the reporters for *USA Today*, Nichols, Hall and Eisler.

The affair was a master stroke: the trap of the American dream
has been skilfully by-passed since Jose Padilla was a stranger and
an alien by his own, free American's, *choice*. And the terrorism
was vividly depicted as simultaneously of foreign origin yet ubiquitous at home, lurking beyond every corner and spreading over
every neighbourhood – just like 'the Reds under the beds' of yore;
and so it was an impeccable metaphor and a fully credible outlet
for the equally ubiquitous fears and apprehensions of precarious
life.

And yet this particular expedient proved to be an error. When
viewed from the other offices of the federal administration, the
assets of the case looked more like liabilities. A 'frighteningly easy
to assemble' 'dirty bomb' would expose the folly of a multibillion-
dollar 'anti-missile shield'. The native credentials of al-Mujahir
could attach a huge question mark to the planned anti-Iraq cru-
sade and all its as yet unnamed sequels. What was meat to some
federal departments smacked of poison to some others. Those
others seem at the moment to have got the upper hand, since the
neck of the promising affair has been promptly, swiftly and expeditiously wrung. But not for the lack of trying on the part of its
authors...

**Modernity turned out and kept on turning out, from the start,
huge volumes of human waste.**

The production of human waste was particularly profuse in two
branches of modern industry (still fully operative and working to
capacity).

The manifest function of the first of the two branches was the
production and reproduction of social order. Any model of order is
selective and requires the cutting off, trimming, segregating, separating or excising of such parts of the human raw material as are
unfit for the new order: unable or not allowed to fill any of its
niches. At the other end of the order-building process, such parts
emerge as 'waste', as distinct from the 'useful', because intended,
product.

The second branch of modern industry known continuously to turn out vast volumes of human waste was economic progress – which requires in turn the incapacitation, dismantling and eventually the annihilation of a certain number of ways and means of eking out a human existence: such livelihoods as cannot and would not meet the constantly rising standards of productivity and profitability. Practitioners of the devaluated forms of life cannot, as a rule, be accommodated *en masse* in the new, slimmer and smarter arrangements for economic activity. They are denied access to such means of livelihood as the new arrangements have made legitimate/obligatory, while the orthodox means, now devalued, no longer offer survival. They are, for that reason, the waste of economic progress.

The potentially disastrous consequences of the accumulation of human waste were, however, for a better part of modern history defused, neutralized or at least mitigated thanks to another modern innovation: the waste-disposal industry. That industry thrived thanks to large parts of the globe being turned into dumping grounds to which all the 'surplus of humanity', the human waste turned out in the modernizing sectors of the planet, could be transported, disposed of and decontaminated – thereby staving off the danger of self-combustion and explosion.

The planet is currently running out of such dumping grounds; in large part because of the spectacular success – the planetary spread – of the modern form of life (at least from the time of Rosa Luxemburg, modernity has been suspected of an ultimately suicidal, 'a snake eating its own tail'-style tendency). Dumping grounds are in ever shorter supply. While the production of human waste goes on unabated (if anything rising in volume due to globalization processes), the waste-disposal industry has found itself in dire straits. Such ways of tackling human waste as have become the modern tradition are no longer feasible, and new ways have not been invented, let alone put into operation. Along the fault-lines of world disorder piles of human waste are rising, and the first signs multiply of the tendency towards self-conflagration and the symptoms of imminent explosion.

The crisis of the human waste-disposal industry stands behind the present-day confusion, revealed by the desperate, though largely irrational and off-the-mark crisis-management bustle triggered on 11 September.

More than two centuries ago, in 1784, Kant observed that the planet we inhabit is a sphere, and thought through the consequences of that admittedly banal fact: as we all stay and move on the surface of that sphere, Kant observed, we have nowhere else to go and hence are bound to live forever in each other's neighbourhood and company. Keeping a distance, let alone lengthening it, is in the long run out of the question: moving round the spherical surface will end up shortening the distance one had tried to stretch. And so *die volkommene bürgerliche Vereinigung in der Menschengattung* (a perfect unification of the human species through common citizenship) is the destiny that Nature chose for us by putting us on the surface of a spherical planet. The unity of humankind is the ultimate horizon of our universal history; a horizon that we, human beings, prompted and guided by reason and the instinct of self-preservation, are bound to pursue, and in the fullness of time reach. Sooner or later, Kant warned, there will not be a scrap of empty space left where those of us who have found the places already occupied too cramped or too inhospitable for comfort, too awkward or for whatever other reason uncongenial, could seek shelter or rescue. And so Nature commands us to view (reciprocal) hospitality as the supreme precept we need to – and eventually will have to – embrace and obey in order to bring to an end the long chain of trials and errors, the catastrophes the errors cause and the devastations the catastrophes leave in their wake.

Kant's readers could learn all that from his book two centuries ago. The world, though, took little notice. It seems that the world prefers to honour its philosophers with memorial plaques rather than by listening to them attentively, let alone by following the advice it hears. Philosophers might have been the main heroes of the Enlightenment lyrical drama, but the post-Enlightenment epic tragedy all but neglected their lines.

Busy with arranging marriages of nations with states, states with sovereignty, and sovereignty with territories surrounded by tightly sealed and vigilantly controlled borders, the world seemed to pursue a horizon quite different from the one Kant had drawn. For 200 years the world was occupied with making the control of human movements the sole prerogative of state powers, with erecting barriers to all other, uncontrolled human movements, and manning the barriers with watchful and heavily armed guards. Passports, entry and exit visas, and customs and immigration controls were prime inventions of the art of modern government.

The advent of the modern state coincided with the emergence of 'stateless persons', the *sans papiers*, and the idea of *unwertes Leben*, the latter-day reincarnation[5] of the ancient institution of *homo sacer*, that ultimate embodiment of the sovereign right to exempt and to exclude any human being who has been cast beyond the limits of human and divine laws, and to make them into a being to whom no laws apply and whose destruction brings no punishment while being devoid of all ethical or religious significance.

The ultimate sanction of the modern sovereign power turned out to be the right of exemption from humanity.

A few years after Kant had written down his conclusions and sent them to the printers, another, even shorter document was published – one that was to weigh on the next two centuries of history and on the minds of its principal actors much more heavily than Kant's little book. That other document was *Déclaration des droits de l'homme et du citoyen*, of which Giorgio Agamben would observe, with the benefit of hindsight across two centuries, that it did not make it clear whether 'the two terms [*man* and *citizen*] were to name two distinct realities' or whether, instead, the first term was always meant to be 'already contained in the second'[6] – that is, the bearer of rights was the man who was also (or in as far as he was) a citizen.

That lack of clarity, with all its gruesome consequences, had been noted before by Hannah Arendt – in a world suddenly filling up with 'displaced persons'. Arendt recalled the old and genuinely prophetic Edmund Burke's premonition that the abstract naked-ness of 'being nothing but human' was humanity's greatest danger.[7] 'Human rights', as Burke noted, were an abstraction, and humans could expect little protection from 'human rights' unless the abstraction was filled with the flesh of the Englishman's or a Frenchman's rights. 'The world found nothing sacred in the abstract nakedness of being human' – so Arendt summed up the experience of the years that followed Burke's observations. 'The Rights of Man, supposedly inalienable, proved to be unen-forceable...whenever people appeared who were no longer citi-zens of any sovereign state.'[8]

Indeed, human beings endowed with 'human rights' but with nothing more than that – with no other, more defensible since better institutionally rooted rights to contain and hold 'human' rights in place – were nowhere to be found and to all practical intents unimaginable. A social, all-too-social, *puissance, potenza, might* or *Macht*[9] was obviously needed to endorse the humanity of humans. And throughout the modern era, such 'potency' happened to be, invariably, the potency *to draw a boundary be-tween human and inhuman, in modern times disguised as the boundary between citizens and foreigners.* On this earth sliced into estates of sovereign states, the homeless are rightless, and they suffer not because they are not equal before the law – but because *there is no law that applies to them* and to which they could refer in their complaints against the rough deal they have been accorded, or to whose protection they could lay claim.

In her essay on Karl Jaspers penned a few years after *The Origins of Totalitarianism*, Hannah Arendt observed that al-though for all preceding generations 'humanity' had been but a concept or an ideal (we may add: a philosophical postulate, a humanists' dream, sometimes a war-cry, but hardly ever the organizing principle of political action), it had 'become something of an urgent reality'.[10] It had become a matter of extreme urgency because the impact of the West had not only saturated the rest of the world with the products of its technological development, but it had also exported to the rest of the world 'its processes of disintegration' – among them the breakdown of metaphysical and religious beliefs, awesome advances of natural sciences and the ascendance of the nation-state as virtually the sole form of government figured most prominently. The forces which had required long centuries to 'undermine the ancient beliefs and political ways of life' in the West 'took only a few decades to break down... beliefs and ways of life in all other parts of the world'.

This kind of unification, Arendt suggests, could not but produce a kind of 'solidarity of mankind' that is 'entirely negative'. Each part of the human population of the earth is made vulnerable by all other parts, and each of the other parts. This is, we may say, a 'solidarity' of dangers, risks and fears. For most of the time and in the thoughts of most, the 'unity of the planet' boils down to the horror of threats gestating or incubated in distant parts of the world – a world 'reaching out yet itself out of reach'.

Every factory turns out waste alongside its intended product. The factory of territorially grounded modern sovereignty was no exception.

For 200 years or so after the publication of Kant's musings, the progressive 'filling of the world' (and so, consequently, the urge to admit that the fullness of the planet Kant thought to be an unavoidable verdict of Reason and Nature rolled into one, with no appeal allowed, was indeed eminent) was fought back with the help of the (un)holy trinity of territory, nation, and state.

Nation-state, as Giorgio Agamben observes, is a state that makes 'nativity or birth' the 'foundation of its own sovereignty'. 'The fiction that is implicit here', Agamben points out, 'is that *birth* [*nascita*] comes into being immediately as *nation*, so that there may not be any difference between the two moments.'[11] One is, so to speak, *born* into the 'citizenship of the state'.

The nakedness of the newly born child as yet unwrapped in legal/juridical trappings provides the site on which the sovereignty of state power is constructed and perpetually rebuilt and serviced with the help of the practices of inclusion/exclusion aimed at all other claimants of citizenship who happen to fall within the reach of the state's sovereignty. We may hypothesize that the reduction of *bios* to *zoë* which Agamben takes as the essence of modern sovereignty (or, we may say as well, the reduction of the *Leib*, the living-acting body, to the *Körper*, a body that can be acted upon but cannot act) is a foregone conclusion once birth is selected as the only 'natural', no-questions-asked and no tests required, entry into the nation.

All other claimants who may knock at the door of the sovereign state asking to be admitted tend first to be submitted to the derobing ritual. As Victor Turner suggested, following Van Gennep's three-stage scheme of *rite de passage*, before newcomers applying for admission to a social site are given access (if access is given) to that new wardrobe where the dresses appropriate to the new site and reserved for that site are stocked, they need to be stripped (metaphorically as well as literally) of all and any trappings of their previous assignment. They must remain for a while in a state of 'social nakedness'. The quarantine is spent in a non-space of 'betwixt and between', where no clothes of socially defined and approved significance are on offer and none are permitted. A purgatory of the intermediate 'nowhere space' that separates the plots in a world sliced into plots and conceived as an aggregation of spatially separate plots separates the newcomers from their new belonging. Inclusion, if it is to be offered, must be preceded by a radical exclusion.

According to Turner, the message conveyed by the obligatory stopover on a camping site thoroughly cleansed of any implements capable of lifting the campers from the level of *zoë* or *Körper* to that of *bios* or *Leib* ('the social significance of rendering them down into some kind of human *primo materia*, divested of specific form and reduced to a condition that, although it is still social, is without or beneath all accepted forms of status') is that there is no direct path leading from one to another socially approved status. Before one can pass from one status to another, one needs to be immersed and to dissolve in 'an unstructured or rudimentarily structured and relatively undifferentiated *communitas*...'[12]

Hannah Arendt situated the phenomenon later explored by Turner in the power-operated realm of expulsion, exile, exclusion and exemption. Humanity that takes 'the form of fraternity', she implied, 'is the great privilege of pariah peoples' – who in the public debates of the eighteenth century were talked about under the generic name of *les malheureux*, in those of the nineteenth century were rebranded as *les misérables*, and today, since the middle of the past century, are crowded under the umbrella notion of 'the refugees' – but have been at all times deprived of a place of their own on the mental map of the world drawn by the people who coined and deployed their names. Rammed, cramped and crushed by multiple rejections, 'the persecuted have moved so closely together that the inter-space which we have called world (and which of course existed between them before the persecution, keeping them at a distance from one another) has simply disappeared.'[13]

For all practical intents and purposes the pariah/outcast categories were *out of the world*: the world of categories and fine distinctions which the powers that be had spawned and made known under the name of 'society' – the only world humans were supposed to inhabit and the only world that could reforge its denizens into citizens, the bearers and practitioners of rights. They were *uniform* – in their common lack of attributes of a kind that vernacular speakers would be able to note, grasp, name and comprehend. Or at least 'uniform' was what they seemed to be – due to the alliance between the poverty of the vernacular and the power-assisted homogenization through expropriation of rights.

If birth and nation are one, then all the others who enter or wish to enter the national family must mimic, or are compelled to emulate, the nakedness of the newborn.

The state – the guardian and prison guard, the spokesman and the censor-in-chief of the nation – would see to it that this condition was met.

As Carl Schmitt, arguably a most clear-headed, illusion-free anatomist of the modern state, avers: 'He who determines a value, *eo ipso* always fixes a nonvalue. The sense of this determination of a nonvalue is the annihilation of the nonvalue.'[14] Determining the value draws the limits of the normal, the ordinary, the orderly. Non-value is an exception that marks this boundary.

The exception is that which cannot be subsumed; it defies general codification, but it simultaneously reveals a specifically juridical formal element: the decision in absolute purity...There is no rule that is applicable to chaos. Order must be established for juridical order to make sense. A regular situation must be created, and sovereign is he who definitely decides if this situation is actually effective...The exception does not only confirm the rule; the rule as such lives off the exception alone.[15]

Giorgio Agamben comments: 'The rule applies to the exception in no longer applying, in withdrawing from it. The state of exception is thus not the chaos that preceded order but rather the situation that results from its suspension. In this sense, the exception is truly, according to its etymological root, *taken outside* (*ex-capere*), and not simply excluded.'[16]

Let me observe that this is precisely the circumstance which the rule-making sovereigns, to legitimize and see through their actions, need to occlude. Order-making tends to be, as a rule, undertaken in the name of fighting chaos. But there would be no chaos were there no ordering intention already in place and were not the 'regular situation' already conceived in advance so that its promotion could start in earnest. Chaos is born as a non-value, an exception. The bustle of ordering is its birthplace – and it has no other *legitimate* parents or family home.

The power of exemption would not be a mark of sovereignty were the sovereign power not wedded first to the territory.

Penetrating and insightful as he is when scrutinizing the bizarre, paradoxical logic of *Ordnung*, Carl Schmitt endorses the fiction cultivated by the guardians/promoters of order, the wielders of the sovereign power of exception, on this crucial point. Just as in the body of practice of sovereigns, so in Schmitt's theoretical model the boundaries of the territory over which the work of *Ordnung* is conducted are presumed to constitute the outer limits of the world endowed with topical relevance for the ordering intentions and efforts.

In Schmitt's vision, just as in the *doxa* of lawmakers, the sum total of the resources required to have the ordering job done, as well as the totality of factors necessary to account for its operation and effects, are contained inside that world. Sovereignty produces the distinction between a value and a non-value, a rule and an exception – but this operation is preceded by *the distinction between the inside and the outside of the sovereign realm*, without which the sovereign prerogatives neither could be claimed nor would be obtained. Sovereignty, as practised by the modern nation-state and as theorized by Schmitt, is inextricably bound to a *territory*. Sovereignty is unthinkable without an 'outside'; it is inconceivable in any form other than a *localized* entity. Schmitt's vision is as 'localized' as the sovereignty whose mystery it aims to unravel. It does not step beyond the practice and cognitive horizon of the made-in-heaven wedlock of territory and power.

As the 'state of law' was gradually, but irresistibly (since under constant pressures of legitimacy-building and ideological mobilization) evolving into the 'nation's state', the wedlock has grown into a *ménage à trois*: a trinity – of territory, state and nation. One may suppose that the advent of that trinity was a historical accident that occurred in one, relatively small part of the globe; but since that part, however small, happened to claim the position of a metropolis resourceful enough to transform the rest of the globe into a periphery, and arrogant enough to pointedly overlook or denigrate its own peculiarities, and since it is the prerogative of a metropolis to set the rules by which the periphery should live, and since it is in the metropolis's power to enforce the observance of those rules – the overlap/blend of the nation, state and territory has become a globally binding norm.

Any one of the trinity's members, if unallied with and unsupported by the other two, turned into an anomaly: into a monstrosity bound to undergo drastic surgery or to receive a *coup de grâce* in the event it was perceived as beyond redemption. Territory with no nation-state became a no man's land; nation without a state became a freak given the choice of voluntary disappearance or execution; a state without a nation or with more than one nation turned into a residue of time past or a mutant faced with the option of modernizing or perishing. Behind the new normality loomed the sense-giving principle of territoriality for any power bidding for sovereignty and for all power standing a chance of the bid being granted or won.

All bids for purity sediment dirt, all bids for order create monsters. The dirty monsters of the era of the promotion of the territory/nation/state trinity were nations without states, states with more than one nation, and territory without a nation-state. It was thanks to the threat and fear of those monsters that the sovereign power could claim and acquire the right to deny rights and set such conditions for humanity as a great part of humanity, as it happened, could not meet.

Sovereignty being the power to define the limits of humanity, the lives of those humans who have fallen or have been thrown outside those limits are unworthy of being lived.

In 1920 a booklet was published under the title *Die Freigabe der Vernichtung lebensunwerten Leben* (Allowing the destruction of life unworthy of living), authored by a penal law expert, Karl Binding, and a professor of medicine, Alfred Hoche, and commonly credited with the introduction of the concept of *unwertes leben* ('life unworthy of living') – complete with the suggestion that in known human societies life of this sort has been thus far unduly and unjustly protected at the expense of fully fledged kinds of life that should command all the attention and loving care owed to humanity. The learned authors saw no reason (whether juridical, social or religious) why the extermination of *unwertes Leben* should be seen as a crime and so liable to punishment.

In that Binding/Hoche conception Giorgio Agamben spies out resuscitation and an updated, modern articulation of the ancient category of *homo sacer*: of a human who can be killed without fear of punishment but cannot be used in religious sacrifice; who in other words is exempted absolutely – standing beyond the confines of both human and divine law. Agamben also observes that the concept of 'life unworthy of being lived' is – as the concept of *homo sacer* always was – non-ethical; but that in its modern rendition it acquires profound political significance as a category 'on which sovereign power is founded'.

> In modern biopolitics, sovereign is he who decides on the value or the nonvalue of life as such. Life – which with the declaration of rights, had as such been invested with the principle of sovereignty – now itself becomes the place of a sovereign decision.[17]

This seems to be, indeed, the case. Let us note, though, that it could only be the case in as far as the territory/state/nation trinity has been lifted to the rank of the universal principle of human cohabitation, imposed on and bound to bind every nook and cranny of the planet, including areas that for centuries failed to meet the elementary conditions of such a trinity (that is, homogeneity of the population and/or permanent settlement resulting in a 'rootedness in the soil'). It is because of that contrived, arbitrary and enforced universality of the trinitarian principle that, as Hannah Arendt points out, 'whoever was thrown out of one of these tightly organized communities found himself *thrown* out of the family of nations altogether'[18] (and so also, as the human species became identical with the 'family of nations', from the realm of humanity) into the nowhere-land of *homini sacri.*

The intense production of waste requires an efficient waste-disposal industry; and indeed, this has become one of the most impressive success stories of modern times – which explains why Kant's warning/premonition was able to gather dust for two centuries.

Despite its rising volumes and deepening pains, the human detritus sedimented by the zeal and bustle to include/exclude triggered and consistently reinforced by the principle and the practice of the territory/nation/state trinity could be legitimately played down as a transient and essentially curable irritant, rather than be seen and treated as a portent of an imminent catastrophe. Dark clouds seemed lighter and dark premonitions could be laughed away as 'prophecies of doom' – thanks mostly to the modern enterprise which went down in history under the names of 'imperialism' and 'colonization'. That enterprise served, alongside its other functions, as a disposal and recycling plant for the growing supplies of human waste. The breathtakingly vast expanses of the 'virgin land' laid open for colonization by the imperialist drive to invade, conquer and annexe could be used as a dumping ground for those who were unwanted at home, and act as a promised land for those who fell off or were thrown over board as the vehicle of progress picked up speed and gained ground.

Then, the world seemed anything but full. 'Full' is another – 'objectified' – expression for the feeling of being crowded. *Over-crowded*, to be precise.

No more Statues of Liberty promising to gather in the down-trodden and abandoned masses. No more escape tracks and hide-outs for anyone but a few misfits and criminals. But (this being, arguably, the most striking effect of the world's newly revealed fullness) no more safe and cosy *chez soi* either, as the events of 11 September have proved dramatically and beyond reasonable doubt.

Colonization allowed Kant's premonitions to gather dust. How-ever, it also made them look, when they were finally dusted off, like a prophecy of an apocalypse instead of the cheerful utopia Kant intended them to be. Kant's vision now looks that way because, due to the misleading abundance of 'no man's land', nothing had to be done and thus nothing was done in the course of those two centuries to prepare humanity for the revelation of the ultimate fullness of the world.

As the last spots bearing *ubi leones* tags quickly vanish from the world map and the last among many distant frontier-land territor-ies are claimed by powers potent enough to seal the borders and deny entry visas – *the world in its entirety is turning into a planetary frontier-land . . .*

Frontier-lands of all times have been known as, simultaneously, factories of displacement and recycling plants for the displaced. Nothing else can be expected from their new, global variety – except of course the new, planetary scale of the production and recycling problems.

Let me repeat: there are no local solutions to global problems – although it is precisely local solutions that are avidly sought, though in vain, by the extant political institutions, the sole political institutions that we have collectively invented thus far and the only ones we have.

Embroiled as these institution have been from the start and throughout their history in passionate (Herculean in intention, Sisyphean in practice) efforts to seal the union of state and nation with territory, it is no wonder that all such institutions have become and have remained local, and that their sovereign power to take feasible (or, indeed, *legitimate*) action is locally circumscribed.

Spattered all around the globe are 'garrisons of extraterritoriality', the dumping grounds for the undisposed of and as yet unrecycled waste of the global frontier-land.

During the two centuries of modern history, people who failed to make it into citizens, the refugees, the voluntary and involuntary migrants, 'displaced persons' *tout court*, were naturally assumed to be the host country's affair and handled as such.

Few if any of the nation-states that filled the map of the modern world were as locally entrenched as their sovereign prerogatives. Sometimes willingly, some other times reluctantly, virtually all of them had to accept the presence of aliens inside the appropriated territory, and admit the successive waves of immigrants escaping or chased away from the realms of other sovereign nation-state powers. Once inside, however, settled and brand-new aliens alike fell under the exclusive and undivided jurisdiction of the host country. That country was free to deploy updated, modernized versions of the two strategies which have been described in *Tristes tropiques* by Claude Lévi-Strauss as the alternative ways of dealing with the presence of strangers; when choosing to resort to such strategies it could count on the wholehearted support of all other sovereign powers of the planet, mindful to preserve the inviolability of the territory/nation/state trinity.

The available choice was between the anthropophagic and the anthropoemic solutions to the stranger problem. The first solution boiled down to 'eating the strangers up'. Either literally, in flesh – as in cannibalism allegedly practised by certain ancient tribes – or in its sublimated, spiritual version, as in the power-assisted cultural assimilation practised almost universally by nation-states with the intention of ingesting the carriers of alien culture into the national body while dumping off the indigestible parts of their cultural dowry. The second solution meant 'vomiting the strangers' instead of devouring them: rounding them up and expelling them (just what Oriana Fallaci – the formidable Italian journalist and opinion-maker – suggested we, the Europeans, should do with people who adore other gods and display baffling toilet habits) either from the realm of the state's power or from the world of the living.

Let us note however that pursuing either of these two solutions made sense only on twin assumptions: of a clean-cut territorial division between the 'inside' and the 'outside'; and of the completeness and indivisibility of sovereignty of the strategy-selecting power inside its realm. Neither of the two assumptions commands much credibility today, in our liquid modern global world; and so the chances of deploying either of the two orthodox strategies are, to say the least, slim.

With the tested ways of acting being no longer available, we seem to be left without a good strategy to handle newcomers. In times when no cultural model can authoritatively and effectively claim its superiority over competing models, and when nation-building and patriotic mobilization have ceased to be the principal instruments of social integration and the state's self-assertion, cultural assimilation is no longer on the cards. Since deportations and expulsion make dramatic and rather disturbing television and are likely to trigger a public outcry and tarnish the international credentials of the perpetrators, most governments prefer to steer clear of the trouble if they can, by locking the doors against all who knock asking for shelter.

The present trend of drastically reducing the right to political asylum, accompanied by a stout refusal of entry to 'economic migrants' (except at the few and transient moments when business threatens to travel where labour is, unless labour is brought where business wants it to be), does not signal a new strategy regarding the refugee phenomenon – but the *absence of strategy*, and the wish to avoid a situation in which that absence causes political embarrassment. Under the circumstances, the terrorist assault of 11 September helped the politicians enormously. In addition to the charges usually brandished of sponging on the nation's welfare and stealing jobs,[19] or of bringing into the country long forgotten diseases like tuberculosis or freshly invented ones like HIV,[20] refugees can now stand accused of playing a 'fifth column' role on behalf of the global terrorist network. At long last there is a 'rational' and morally unassailable reason to round up, incarcerate and deport people whom one no longer knows how to handle and for whom one does not want to take the trouble to find out. In the US, and soon after in Britain, under the banner of the 'anti-terrorist campaign', foreigners have been promptly deprived of essential human rights that had until now withstood all the vicissitudes of history since the Magna Carta and Habeas Corpus. Foreigners can now be indefinitely detained on charges against which they cannot defend themselves since they are not told what they are. As Martin Thomas acidly observes,[21] from now on, in a dramatic reversal of the basic principle of civilized law, the 'proof of a criminal charge is a redundant complication' – at least as far as foreign refugees are concerned.

The doors may be locked; but the problem won't go away, however tight the locks. Locks do nothing to tame or weaken the forces that cause displacement and make humans into refugees. The locks may help to keep the problem out of sight and out of mind, but they can not force it out of existence.

And so, increasingly, refugees find themselves in a cross-fire; more exactly, in a double-bind.

They are expelled by force or frightened into fleeing out of their native countries, but refused entry to any other. They do not *change* places; they *lose* place on earth, they are catapulted into a nowhere, into Augé's 'non-lieux' or Garreau's 'nowherevilles', into Michel Foucault's 'Narrenschiffen', into a drifting 'place without a place, that exists by itself, that is closed in on itself and at the same time is given over to the infinity of the sea'[22] – or (as Michel Agier suggests in a forthcoming article in *Ethnography*) in a desert, by

138

definition an *un*inhabited land, a land resentful of humans and seldom visited by them.

Refugees have become, in a caricatured likeness of the new power elite of the globalized world, the epitome of that extraterritoriality where the roots of the present-day *precarité* of the human condition, that foremost of present-day human fears and anxieties, are sunk. Those fears and anxieties, seeking other outlets in vain, have rubbed off on the popular resentment and fear of refugees. They cannot be defused or dispersed in a direct confrontation with the other embodiment of extraterritoriality, the global elite drifting beyond the reach of human control, too powerful to be confronted. Refugees, by contrast, are a sitting target for the unloading of surplus anguish...

According to the office of the UN High Commissioner for Refugees (UNHCR) there are between 13 and 18 million 'victims of enforced displacement' struggling for survival beyond the boundaries of their countries of origin (not counting the millions of 'internal' refugees in Burundi and Sri Lanka, Colombia and Angola, Sudan and Afghanistan, condemned to vagrancy by endless tribal wars). Of those, more than 6 million are in Asia, 7 to 8 million in Africa; there are 3 million Palestinian refugees in the Middle East. This is, to be sure, a conservative estimate. Not all refugees have been recognized (or claimed to be recognized) as such; only so many of the displaced persons were lucky enough to find themselves on the UNHCR register and under their care.

Wherever they go, refugees are unwanted, and left in no doubt that they are. The admittedly 'economic migrants' (that is, people who follow the precepts of 'rational choice' and so try to find a livelihood where it can be found rather than staying where there is none) are openly condemned by the same governments that try hard to make 'flexibility of labour' the prime virtue of their electorate and that exhortate their native unemployed 'to get on their bikes' and go where the buyers of labour are. But the suspicion of economic motives also spills over on those newcomers who not so long ago were seen as exercising their human rights in seeking shelter from discrimination and persecution. Through repeated association, the term 'asylum seeker' has acquired a derogatory flavour. Much of the time and brain capacity of statesmen of the 'European Union' is deployed in designing ever more sophisticated ways of plugging and fortifying borders, and the most expedient procedures to get rid of seekers after bread and shelter who have managed to cross the borders nevertheless.

David Blunkett, the British Home secretary, not to be outdone, has proposed to blackmail the countries of origin of the refugees into taking back the 'disqualified asylum seekers' by cutting financial aid to countries that don't.[23] This was not the sole new idea. Blunkett wishes to 'force the pace of change', complaining that due to the lack of verve among other European leaders, 'progress has still been too slow.' He wants the creation of an all-European 'rapid joint operations force' and 'a taskforce of national experts' to 'draw up common risk assessments identifying weak points in the EU... external borders, addressing the issue of seaborne illegal migration and tackling human trafficking [the new term designed to replace the once noble concept of "passage"]'.

With the active cooperation of governments and other public figures who find in the aiding and abetting of popular prejudices the sole available substitute for confronting the genuine sources of existential uncertainty haunting their electors, the 'asylum seekers' (like those who gather force in the innumerable Sangattes of Europe preparing for the invasion of the British Isles, or those about to settle, unless stopped, in made-to-order camps a few miles from the electors' homes) replace the evil-eyed witches, ghosts of unrepentant evil-doers and other malignant spooks and hobgoblins of urban legends. The new and rapidly swelling urban folklore, with the victims of this planetary casting out in the role of principal ill-intentioned actors, gathers in and recycles the lore of hair-raising horror stories that met an avid demand in the past, generated by the insecurities of city life, just as it is now.

Those migrants who despite the most ingenious of stratagems cannot be expeditiously deported, the government proposes to confine to camps built in possibly remote and isolated parts of the country – a step that transforms into a self-fulfilling prophecy the belief that the migrants do not want to be or cannot be assimilated into the economic life of the country – so, as Gary

Younge observes, 'effectively erecting Bantustans around the British countryside, corralling refugees in ways that will leave them isolated and vulnerable'.[24] (Asylum seekers, as Younge points out, 'are more likely to be victims of crime than perpetrators'.)

Of those refugees on the UNHCR register, 83.2 per cent of those in Africa are placed in camps, and 95.9 per cent of those in Asia. In Europe so far only 14.3 per cent of the refugees have been locked in camps. But there is little sign of hope so far that the difference in favour of Europe will be upheld for long.

The camps of refugees or asylum seekers are artifices of temporary installation made permanent through blocking their exits.

The inmates of the camps of refugees or asylum seekers cannot go back 'where they came from', as the countries they left do not want them back, their livelihoods have been destroyed and their homes have been gutted, razed or stolen. But there is no road forward either: no government would gladly see an influx of homeless millions, and any government would do its best to prevent the newcomers from settling.

As to their new 'permanently temporary' location, the refugees are 'in it, but not of it'. They do not truly belong to the country on whose territory their Portakabins have been assembled or tents pitched. From the rest of the host country, they are separated by an invisible, but all the same thick and impenetrable veil of suspicion and resentment. They are suspended in a spatial void in which time has ground to a halt. They have neither settled, nor are they on the move; they are neither sedentary nor nomadic.

In the habitual terms in which human identities are narrated, they are *ineffable*. They are Jacques Derrida's 'undecidables' made flesh. Among people like us, praised by others and priding ourselves for the arts of reflection and self-reflection, they are not only un*touch*ables, but un*think*ables. In a world filled to the brim with imagined communities, they are the *unimaginables*. And it is by refusing them the right to be imagined that the others, assembled in genuine or hoping-to-become-genuine communities, seek credibility for their own labours of the imagination.

141

The proliferation of refugee camps is as integral a product/manifestation of globalization as the dense archipelago of stopover *nowherevilles* through which the members of the new globetrotting elite move on their round-the-world voyages.

The attribute which the globetrotters and the refugees share is their *extraterritoriality*: their not truly belonging to the place, being 'in' but not 'of' the space they physically occupy (the globetrotters in a succession of admittedly fleeting moments, the refugees in an infinitely extended series of moments).

For all we know, the *nowherevilles* of the locked-up refugee camps, not unlike the halfway inns of the freely travelling supranational traders, may be the bridgeheads of an advancing extraterritoriality, or (in a longer perspective) laboratories in which the desemanticization of place, the frailty and disposability of meanings, the indeterminacy and plasticity of identities, and above all the new *permanence of transience* (all constitutive tendencies of the 'liquid' phase of modernity) are experimented with under extreme conditions: tested in a way similar to that in which the limits of human pliability and submissiveness, and the ways of reaching such limits, were tested in the concentration camps of the 'solid' stage of modern history.

Like all the other *nowherevilles*, refugee camps are marked by an intended, preprogrammed and in-built transience. All such installations are conceived and planned as a hole in time as much as in space, a temporary suspension of the time sequence of identity building and territorial ascription. But the faces which the two varieties of *nowhereville* show to their respective users/inmates differ sharply. The two kinds of extraterritoriality sediment, so to speak, on the opposite sides of the globalizing process.

The first offers transience as a facility chosen at will; the second makes it permanent – an irrevocable and ineluctable fate. This is a difference not unlike that which separates the two outfits of secure permanence: the gated communities of discriminating rich, and the ghettos of discriminated poor. And the causes of difference are also similar: entries closely guarded and watched but exits wide open on the one side; and entry largely indiscriminate but exits tightly sealed on the other. It is the locking of exits in particular that perpetuates the state of transience without replacing it with permanence. In refugee camps time is barred to qualitative change. It is still time, but no longer history.

Refugee camps boast a new quality: a 'frozen transience', an ongoing, lasting state of temporary-ness, a duration patched together of moments none of which is lived through as an element of, let alone a contribution to, perpetuity. For the inmates of refugee camps, the prospect of long-term sequels and their consequences is not part of the experience. The inmates of refugee camps live, literally, from day to day – and the contents of daily life are unaffected by the knowledge that days combine into months and years. As in the prisons and 'hyperghettos' scrutinized and vividly described by Loïc Wacquant,[25] camped refugees 'learn to live, or rather survive [(sur)vivre] from day to day in the immediacy of the moment, bathing in . . . the despair brewing inside the walls'.

The rope fixing the refugees to their camps is plaited of push and pull forces.

The powers ruling over the site on which the tents were pitched or the barracks assembled, and over the land around the camp, do whatever they can to prevent the camp inmates from leaking out and spilling over the adjacent territory. Even in the absence of armed guards at the exits, the outside of the camp is, essentially, off-limits for the camp's insiders. At the very best it is inhospitable, full of wary, unsympathetic and suspicious people eager to note, record and hold against the inmates any genuine or putative error and every false step the refugees may take – the kinds of steps that the refugees, having been chased out of their element and ill at ease in an unfamiliar environment, are only too likely to take.

In the land where their temporary/permanent tents have been pitched, refugees remain blatantly the 'outsiders', a threat to the security which the 'established' draw from their heretofore unquestioned daily routine. They are a challenge to the heretofore universally shared worldview and a source of dangers not yet confronted, fitting ill into the familiar slots and evading the habitual ways of problem-solving.[26]

143

The natives–refugees encounter is, arguable, the most spectacular specimen of the 'established and outsiders dialectics' (one that seems to have gained in our times the pattern-setting role once occupied by the dialectics of master and slave), first described by Elias and Scotson.[27] The 'established', using their power to define the situation and impose their definition on all those involved, tend to enclose the newcomers in an iron cage of stereotype, 'a highly simplified representation of social realities'. Stereotyping creates 'a black and white design' that leaves 'no room for diversities'. The outsiders are guilty until proved innocent, but since it is the established who combine the roles of prosecutors, examining magistrates and judges and so simultaneously make the charges, sit in judgment and pronounce on the truth, the chances of acquittal are slim, if not nil. As Elias and Scotson found out, the more threatened the established population feels, the more their beliefs are likely to be driven 'towards extremes of illusion and doctrinaire rigidity'. And faced with an influx of refugees, the established population has every reason to feel threatened. In addition to representing the 'great unknown' which all strangers embody, the refugees bring home distant noises of war and the stench of gutted homes and scorched villages that cannot but remind the established how easily the cocoon of their safe and familiar (safe *because* familiar) routine may be pierced or crushed. Refugees, as Bertold Brecht pointed out in *Die Landschaft des Exils*, are 'ein Bote des Unglücks' ('a harbinger of ill tidings').

Venturing from the camp to a nearby township, the refugees expose themselves to a kind of uncertainty they find difficult to bear after the stagnant and frozen, but comfortably predictable, day in day out routine of camp life. A few steps from the perimeter of the camp they find themselves in a hostile environment. Their right of entry into 'the outside' is at best a moot question and may be challenged by any passer-by. Compared to such a wilderness outside, the inside of the camp may well pass for a safe haven. Only the reckless and the adventurous would wish to leave it for any considerable time, and fewer yet would dare to act on their wishes.

Using the terms derived from Loïc Wacquant's analyses,[28] we may say that the refugee camps mix, blend and gel together the distinctive features of both the 'community ghetto' of the Ford–Keynes era and the 'hyperghetto' of our post-Fordist and post-Keynesian times. If 'community ghettos' were relatively self-sustaining and self-reproducing social quasi-totalities, complete with miniature replicas of the wider society's stratification, functional divisions and institutions designed to serve the complete inventory of the needs of communal life – 'hyperghettos' are anything but self-sustaining communities. They are truncated, artificial and blatantly incomplete groupings of people, aggregates but not communities; topographical condensations unable to survive on their own. Once the elites have managed to run out of the ghetto and have stopped feeding the network of economic ventures that sustained (however precariously) the livelihood of the ghetto population, the agencies of state-managed care and control (the two functions, as a rule, closely intertwined) move in. A 'hyperghetto' is suspended on strings that originate beyond its boundaries and most certainly beyond its control.

Michel Agier found in the refugee camps features of 'community ghettos' intertwined in a tight network of mutual dependency with the attributes of the 'hyperghetto'.[29] We may surmise that such a combination tightens still more strongly the bond tying the inmates to the camp. The pull holding together the denizens of the 'community ghetto' and the push condensing the outcasts into a 'hyperghetto', both powerful forces in their own right, are superimposed and mutually reinforce each other. In combination with the seething and festering hostility of the outside environment, they jointly generate an overwhelming centripetal force, difficult to resist, making all but redundant the techniques of enclosure and isolation developed by the managers and supervisors of Auschwitzes or Gulags. More than any other contrived social microworlds, refugee camps come close to Erving Goffman's ideal type of the 'total institution': they offer, by commission or by omission, a 'total life' from which there is no escape, with access effectively barred to any other form of life.

Having abandoned or been forced out of their former and familiar milieu, refugees tend to be stripped of the identities defined, sustained and reproduced by that milieu.

Socially, they are 'zombies': their old identities survive mostly as ghosts – haunting the nights all the more painfully for being all but invisible in the camp's daylight. Even the most comfortable, prestigious and coveted among their old identities turn into handicaps: they cramp the search for new identities better suited to the new milieu, prevent a coming to grips with new realities, and delay the recognition of the permanence of the new condition.

For all practical intents and purposes, the refugees have been consigned to that intermediate, 'betwixt and between' stage of Van Gennep's and Victor Turner's three-stage passage[30] – but without this consignment having been recognized for what it is, without a time set for its duration, and above all without an awareness that a return to the earlier condition is no longer an option, and with no inkling of the nature of the new settings that may loom ahead. Let us recall that in the tripartite scheme of 'passage' the derobing that took away from the carriers of former roles the social attributes and cultural tokens of the status once enjoyed but now withdrawn (the social, power-assisted production of the 'bare body', as Giorgio Agamben would say[31]) was but a necessary preliminary stage for rerobing the 'socially naked' in the paraphernalia of their new social role. Social (often also bodily) nakedness was but a brief intermezzo separating the two dramatically distinct movements of the life opera – marking the separation between the two successively assumed sets of social rights and obligations. It is different, though, in the case of the refugees. Although their condition bears all the traits (and the consequences) of the social nakedness characteristic of the intermediate, transitory stage of passage (lack of social definition and codified rights and duties), it is neither an intermediate nor a transitory 'stage' leading to some specific, socially defined 'steady state'. In the plight of the refugees, the condition designed as 'intermediateness incarnate' extends indefinitely (a truth that the dramatic fate of the Palestinian refugee camps has recently brought violently into public attention). Whatever 'steady state' may eventually emerge can be only an unplanned and unintended side-effect of the suspended or arrested development – of the fluid, admittedly temporary and experimental attempts at sociation imperceptibly freezing into stiff, no longer negotiable structures, holding the inmates more firmly than any number of armed guards and any amount of barbed wire would.

The permanence of transitoriness; the durability of the transient; the objective determination unreflected in the subjective consequentiality of actions; the perpetually underdefined social role, or more correctly an insertion into the flow of life without an anchor of a social role; all such and related features of liquid modern life have been exposed and documented in Agier's findings. In the refugee camp's territorially fixed extraterritoriality they appear in a form much more extreme, undiluted and so more clearly visible than they do in any other segment of contemporary society.

One wonders to what extent the refugees' camps are laboratories where (unwittingly perhaps, but no less forcefully for that reason) the new liquid modern 'permanently transient' pattern of life is put to the test and rehearsed.

To what extent are the refugees' *nowherevilles* the advanced samples of the world to come, and their inmates cast/pushed/forced into the role of its pioneer explorers? Questions of this kind can only be answered (if at all) in retrospect.

For instance, we can see now – with the benefit of hindsight – that the Jews leaving the ghettos in the nineteenth century were the first to taste and fathom in full the incongruity of the assimilation project and the inner contradictions of the ruling self-assertion precept, later to be experienced by all denizens of emergent modernity. And we begin to see now, again with the benefit of hindsight, that the post-colonial multi-ethnic intelligentsia (like Ralph Singh in Naipaul's *Mimic Men* who could not forget having offered his favourite teacher an apple, like all well-bred English children are supposed to do, though he knew perfectly well that there were no apples on the Caribbean island where the school was) were the first to taste and fathom the fatal flaws, incoherence and lack of cohesion of the identity-building precept that were to be experienced shortly afterwards by the rest of the liquid modern world's inhabitants.

Perhaps the time will arrive for discovering the avant-garde role of the present-day refugees – for exploring the taste of *nowhereville* life and the stubborn permanence of transience that may become the common habitat of the denizens of the globalized, full planet.

Only the kind of community that occupies most of present-day political discourse but cannot be found anywhere else – the *global* community, an inclusive yet not exclusive community matching Kant's vision of *allgemeine Vereinigung in der Menschengattung* – could lift present-day refugees out of the sociopolitical void into which they have been cast.

All communities are imagined. The 'global community' is no exception to that rule. But imagination tends to turn into a tangible, potent, effective integrating force when aided by socially produced and politically sustained institutions of collective self-identification and self-government; this has happened before – in the case of modern nations, wedded for better or worse and till-death-them-do-part to modern sovereign states.

As far as the imagined *global* community is concerned, a similar institutional network (that this time can only be woven of *global* agencies of democratic control, a *globally* binding legal system and *globally* upheld ethical principles) is largely absent. And this, I suggest, is a major, perhaps the principal, cause of that massive production of inhumanity which has been called, euphemistically, the 'refugee problem'. It is also the major obstacle to the resolution of that problem.

At the time Kant jotted down his thoughts on the human, all-human community that Nature had decreed to be the destiny of the human species, universality of individual freedom was the declared purpose and the guiding vision whose advent the men of practice, inspired and closely watched by the men of thought, were expected and prodded to pursue and speed up. Community of mankind and individual freedom were thought of as two faces of the same task (or, yet more to the point, as Siamese twins), since freedom (to quote Alain Finkielkraut's study of the legacy of the twentieth century published under the apt title

148

'The Lost Humanity'[32]) was conceived as tantamount to the 'irreducibility of the individual to his rank, status, community, nation, origins and pedigree'. The fates of the planetary community and of individual freedom were deemed, with good reason, to be inseparable. It was assumed, whenever such a matter was pondered, that *Vereinigung der Menschengattung* and freedom of all its individual members could thrive together or wilt and die together, but never be born alone or survive in separation. Either the membership of the human species overrides all other, more particular assignments and allegiances when it comes to the formulation and allocation of man-made laws and rights – or the cause of human freedom as an inalienable human right is compromised or lost altogether. *Tertium non datur.*

That axiom fast lost its incipient self-evidence and came to be all but forgotten as the humans liberated from confinement in hereditary estates and pedigrees were promptly incarcerated in the new triune prison of the territory/nation/state alliance, while 'human rights' – in political practice, if not in philosophical theory – were redefined as a product of a personal union between subject of the state, member of the nation and legitimate resident of the territory. 'Human community' looks today as remote from current planetary reality as it was at the beginning of the modern adventure. In current visions of the future the place it tends to be assigned, if such an assignment is contemplated at all, is even more distant than two centuries ago. No longer is it seen as imminent or inescapable.

So far, the prospects are bleak.

In his recent sober assessment of the current tendency, David Held finds the affirmation of 'the irreducible moral status of each and every person' and the rejection of 'the view of moral particularists that belonging to a given community limits and determines the moral worth of the individuals and the nature of their freedom' to be tasks that are still outstanding, and widely seen as 'uncomfortable'.[33]

Held notes a few developments inspiring hope (notably the 1948 UN Declaration of Human Rights and the 1998 Statute of the International Criminal Court – though the latter still waits in vain to be ratified and is actively sabotaged by some of the major global players), but observes at the same time 'strong temptations to simply put up the shutters and defend the position of some nations and countries only'. The post-11 September prospects are not particularly encouraging either. They contain a chance to 'strengthen our multilateral institutions and international legal agreements', but there is also a possibility of responses that 'could take us away from these fragile gains toward a world of further antagonisms and divisions – a distinctively uncivil society'. Held's overall summary is anything but optimistic: 'At the time of writing the signs are not good.' Our consolation, though (the only consolation available, but also – let me add – the only one human-kind needs when falling on dark times), is the fact that 'history is still with us and can be made'.

Yes, indeed – history is anything but finished, and choices still can, and inevitably will, be made. One wonders, though, whether the choices already made in the last two centuries have brought us closer to the target envisaged by Kant; or whether, on the contrary, after two centuries of the uninterrupted promotion, entrenchment and ascendance of the Trinitarian Principle we've found ourselves further away from that target than we were at the start of the modern adventure.

> The world is not humane just because it is made by human beings, and it does not become humane just because the human voice sounds in it, but only when it has become the object of discourse ... We humanize what is going on in the world and in ourselves only by speaking of it, and in the course of speaking of it we learn to be human.
> The Greeks called this humanness which is achieved in the discourse of friendship *philanthropia*, 'love of man', since it manifests itself in a readiness to share the world with other men.

These words of Hannah Arendt could be – should be – read as a prolegomena to all future efforts aimed at arresting the reverse drift and bringing history closer to the ideal of 'human commu-nity'. Following Lessing, her intellectual hero, Arendt avers that 'openness to others' is 'the precondition of "humanity" in every sense of the word'...[T]ruly human dialogue differs from mere talk or even discussion in that it is entirely permeated by pleasure in the other person and what he says.'[34] It was the great merit of Lessing, in Arendt's view, that 'he was glad for the sake of the infinite number of opinions that arise when men discuss the affairs of this world.' Lessing

> rejoiced in the very thing that has ever – or at least since Parmenides and Plato – distressed philosophers: that the truth, as soon as it is uttered, is immediately transformed into one opinion among many, is contested, reformulated, reduced to one subject of discourse among others. Lessing's greatness does not merely consist in a theoretical insight that there cannot be one single truth within the human world but in his gladness that it does not exist and that, therefore, the unending discourse among men will never cease as long as there are men at all. A single absolute truth...would have been the death of all those disputes...[a]nd this would have spelled the end of humanity.[35]

The fact that others disagree with us (do not hold dear what we do but instead hold dear what we don't; believe that human togetherness may benefit from being based on other rules than those which we consider superior; above all, doubt our claim of access to a hotline to absolute truth, and so also our bid to know for sure where the discussion must end before it has started) *is not* an obstacle on the road to human community. But our conviction that our opinions *are* the whole truth, nothing but the truth and above all the sole truth that there is, and our belief that other people's truths, if different from ours, are 'mere opinions' – *are* such an obstacle.

Historically, such convictions and such beliefs drew credibility from the material superiority and/or power of resistance of their holders – and the holders in question derived their strength from the entrenchment of the Trinitarian Rule. Indeed, the 'sovereignty complex' entrenched in the (un)holy union of territory, nation and state effectively bars the discourse that Lessing and Arendt took to be the 'precondition of humanity'. It allows the partners/adversaries to load the dice and stack the cards before the game of mutual communication has started, and to break up the debate before the cheat comes dangerously close to being called.

151

The Trinitarian Rule has a self-perpetuating momentum. It confirms its own truth as it gains ascendancy over human lives and minds. A world dominated by that rule is a world of 'nationally frustrated populations', which prodded by their frustration grow convinced that 'true freedom, true emancipation' can be attained only 'with full national emancipation'[36] – that is, through the magic blend of nation with territory and a sovereign state. It was the Trinitarian Rule that caused the frustration, and it is the same rule that offers itself as the remedy. The pain suffered by the outcasts of the territorial/national/state alliance reaches its victims after previous reprocessing in the Trinitarian plant, and it is supplied complete with explanatory brochure and with its foolproof recipe for cure, dressed up as empirically grounded wisdom. In the course of its reprocessing, the alliance is miraculously transmogrified from a curse into a blessing, from the cause of pain into the anaesthetic.

Arendt concludes her essay on 'Humanity in dark times' with a quotation from Lessing: 'Jeder sage, was ihm Wahrheit dünkt,/und die Wahrheit selbst sei Gott empfohlen' ('Let each man say what he deems truth,/and let truth itself be commended unto God').[37]

The Lessing/Arendt message is quite straightforward. Commending the truth to God means leaving the question of truth (the question of 'who is right') open. The truth may only emerge at the far end of conversation – and in a genuine conversation (that is, a conversation that is not a soliloquy in disguise); no partner is certain of knowing, or is able to know, what that end may be (if there is an end, that is). A speaker, and also a thinker who thinks in a 'speaking mode', cannot, as Franz Rosenzweig points out, 'anticipate anything; he must be able to wait because he depends on the word of the other; he requires time.'[38] And as Nathan Glatzer, Rosenzweig's most acute scholar, suggests – there is 'a curious parallel' between Rosenzweig's model of a thinker in the 'speaking mode' and William James's processual/dialogical concept of truth: 'Truth *happens* to an idea. It *becomes* truth, is *made* true by events. Its verity is in fact an event, a process: the process namely of the verifying itself, its veri-*fication*. Its validity is the process of its valid*ation*.'[39] Indeed, affinity is striking – though for Rosenzweig the speech earnestly and hopefully engaged in a dialogue, a speech unsure-of-the-result-of-the-dialogue and therefore unsure-of-its-own-truth, is the principal substance of the 'event' in which truth is 'made', and the principal tool of 'making' it.

Truth is an eminently agonistic concept. It is born of the confrontation between beliefs resistant to reconciliation and between their carriers unwilling to compromise. Short of such a confrontation, the idea of 'truth' would hardly have occurred in the first place. 'Knowing how to go on' would be all one needed to know – and the setting in which one needs 'to go on', unless challenged and thus made 'unfamiliar' and shaken out of its 'self-evidence', tends to come complete with an unambiguous prescription for 'going on'. Disputing *truth* is a response to 'cognitive dissonance'. It is prompted by the urge to devalue and disempower another reading of the setting and/or another prescription for acting that cast doubt on one's own reading and one's own action routine. That urge will grow in intensity the more vociferous and difficult to stifle the objections/obstacles become. The stake in disputing the truth, and the primary purpose of its self-assertion, is proof that the partner/adversary is in the wrong and therefore that the objections are invalid and may be disregarded.

When it comes to disputing truth, the chances for an 'undistorted communication' as postulated by Jürgen Habermas become slim.[40] The protagonists will hardly resist the temptation to resort to other, more effective means than the logical elegance and persuasive power of their arguments. They would rather do whatever they can to render the arguments of the adversary inconsequential, better still inaudible, and best of all never voiced in the first place due to the incapacitation of those who would have voiced them if they could. One argument that will stand the greatest chance of being raised is the ineligibility of the adversary as a partner-in-conversation – due to the adversary being inept, deceitful or otherwise unreliable, harbouring ill intentions or being altogether inferior and substandard.

Were the choice available, refusing conversation or withdrawing from debate would be preferred to arguing the case. Entering argument is, after all, an oblique confirmation of the partner's credentials and a promise to follow the rules and the standards of the (counterfactually) *lege artis* and *bona fide* discourse. Above all, entering argument means, as Lessing pointed out, commending the truth to God; in more down-to-earth terms, it means making the outcome of the debate a hostage to fate. It is safer to declare the adversaries, if possible, *a priori* wrong, and proceed right away to deprive them of the ability to appeal against the verdict, than to attempt to engage in litigation and expose one's own case to cross-examination, therefore risking that it will be disallowed or over-turned.

The expedient of disqualifying an adversary from the truth-debate is most often used by the stronger side; not so much because of its greater iniquity as because of its greater resourcefulness. We may say that the ability to ignore the adversaries and to close one's ears to the causes they promote is the index by which the relative volume and power of resources may be measured. Conversely, going back on the refusal to debate, and agreeing to negotiate the truth is all too often taken for a sign of weakness – a circumstance that makes the stronger side (or one wishing to demonstrate its superior strength) yet more reluctant to abandon its rejectionist stance.

Rejection of Rosenzweig's style of 'speaking thinking' has its own self-perpetuating and self-reinforcing momentum. On the side of the stronger the refusal to talk may pass for a sign of 'being in the right', but for the opposite side the denial of the right to defend its cause entailed by such a refusal, and so by proxy the refusal to recognize its right to be listened to and taken seriously as a bearer of human rights, are the ultimate snubs and humiliations – offences that cannot be taken placidly without loss of human dignity...

Humiliation is a powerful weapon; in addition, it is a boomer-ang-style weapon. It may be resorted to in order to demonstrate or prove the fundamental and irreconcilable inequality between the humiliating and the humiliated sides; but contrary to such intention, it in fact authenticates, veri-*fies* their symmetry, sameness, parity.

154

The measure of humiliation invariably entailed by every act of refusal to converse is not however the sole reason for the refusal to be self-perpetuating. In the frontier-land into which our planet is fast turning as a consequence of one-sided globalization,[41] repeated attempts to overwhelm, disempower and incapacitate the adversary all too often achieve their intended effects, though only with results that go far beyond the perpetrators' anticipation or, for that matter, their liking. Large parts of Africa, Asia or Latin America are covered with lasting traces of past disempowering campaigns: namely, the numerous *local* frontier-lands, side-effects or waste products which the forces benefiting from the conditions of the *global* frontier-land suffer ill, yet which they cannot help sowing and propagating.

The disempowering exercises 'succeed' if the adversary is disarmed beyond hope of recovery – structures of authority are dismantled, social bonds are shredded, the customary sources of livelihood are scorched and put out of operation (in the fashionable political parlance, the territories so afflicted are dubbed 'weak states', though the term 'state', however qualified, can be justified in this case only by being used *sous rature*, as Derrida would say). If supported by a high-tech armoury, words tend to become flesh, and so obliterate their own need and purpose. In local frontier-lands, there is no one left to talk to – QED.

In an Irish joke, a passer-by who is asked by a driver 'how to get from here to Dublin', answers: 'If I wished to go to Dublin, I wouldn't start from here.'

Indeed, one can easily imagine a world better fit for the journey towards Kant's 'universal unity of mankind' than the world we happen to inhabit today, at the far end of the territory/nation/state trinity era. But there is no such alternative world, and so no other site from which to start the journey. And yet not starting it, or not starting it without delay, is – in this one case beyond doubt – *not an option*.

The unity of the human species that Kant postulated may be, as he suggested, resonant with Nature's intention – but it certainly does not seem 'historically determined'. The continuing

155

uncontrollability of the already global network of mutual dependence and 'mutually assured vulnerability' most certainly does not increase the chance of such unity. This only means, however, that at no other time have the keen search for common humanity, and the practice that follows such an assumption, been as urgent and imperative as they are now.

In the era of globalization, the cause and the politics of shared humanity face the most fateful of the many fateful steps they have made in their long history.

Notes

1 Falling In and Out of Love

1 Erich Fromm, *The Art of Loving* (1957; Thorsons, 1995), p. vii.
2 Emmanuel Levinas, *Le Temps et l'autre* (Presses Universitaires de France, 1991), pp. 81, 78.
3 *Guardian Weekend*, 12 Jan. 2002.
4 Adrienne Burgess, *Will You Still Love Me Tomorrow* (Vermilion, 2001), as quoted in *Guardian Weekend*, 26 Jan. 2002.
5 Knud Løgstrup, *Den Etiske Fordring* (Nordisk Forlag, 1956), trans. Theodor I. Jensens as *The Ethical Demand* (University of Notre Dame Press, 1997), pp. 24–5.
6 Fromm, *The Art of Loving*.
7 David L. Norton and Mary F. Kille (eds), *Philosophies of Love* (Helix Books, 1971).
8 Franz Rosenzweig, *Das Büchlein vom gesunden und kranken Menschenverstand*, trans. as *Understanding the Sick and the Healthy*, ed. N. N. Glatzer (Harvard University Press, 1999).
9 *Guardian Weekend*, 9 Mar. 2002.
10 Richard Sennett, *The Fall of Public Man* (1974; Random House, 1978), pp. 259 ff.
11 *Guardian Weekend*, 6 Apr. 2002.

2 In and Out of the Toolbox of Sociality

1 Volkmar Sigusch, 'The neosexual revolution', *Archives of Sexual Behaviour*, 4 (1989), pp. 332–59.

2 Erich Fromm, *The Art of Loving* (1957; Thorsons, 1995).

3 Ibid., pp. 41–3, 9–11.

4 Sigusch, 'The neosexual revolution'.

5 Milan Kundera, *Immortality*, trans. Peter Kussi (Faber, 1991), pp. 338–9.

6 Judith Butler, *Bodies that Matter: On the Discursive Limits of Sex* (Routledge, 1993).

7 Sigmund Freud, '"Civilized" sexual morality and modern nervousness' (1907), here quoted according to James Strachey's Standard Edition of 1959.

8 Jonathan Rowe, 'Reach out and annoy someone', *Washington Monthly*, Nov. 2000.

9 John Urry, 'Mobility and proximity', *Sociology* (May 2002), pp. 255–74.

10 See Émile Durkheim's *The Rules of Sociological Method*, here quoted in Anthony Giddens's translation, *Émile Durkheim: Selected Writings* (Cambridge University Press, 1972), pp. 71, 64.

11 Michael Schluter and David Lee, *The R Factor* (Hodder and Stoughton, 1993), pp. 15, 37.

12 Louise France, 'Love at first site', *Observer Magazine*, 30 June 2002.

13 Jonathan Rowe and Judith Silverstein, 'The GDP myth: why "growth" isn't always a good thing', *Washington Monthly*, Mar. 1999.

14 Here quoted after Jonathan Rowe, 'Z zycia ekonomistow', *Obywatel* 2 (2002); originally published July 1999.

15 For the concept of 'sociality', see my *Postmodern Ethics* (Polity, 1993), p. 119. The juxtaposition of 'sociality' and 'socialization' is parallel to that of 'spontaneity' and 'management'. 'Sociality puts uniqueness above regularity and the sublime above the rational, being therefore generally inhospitable to the rules, rendering the discursive redemption of rules problematic, and cancelling the instrumental meaning of action.'

16 See a remarkably insightful study by Valentina Fedotova, 'Anarkhia i poriadok' (Anarchy and order), *Voprosy Filosofii* 5 (1997), recently reprinted in a collection of the author's studies under the same title (Editorial URSS, 2000), pp. 27–50.

17 Victor Turner, *The Ritual Process: Structure and Anti-structure* (Routledge, 1969), p. 96.

3 On the Difficulty of Loving Thy Neighbour

1 Sigmund Freud, *Civilization and its Discontents* (1930), see James Strachey's Standard Edition, 1961.
2 Knud Ejler Løgstrup, *Etiske Fordring*, here quoted after the English translation, *The Ethical Demand*, ed. Hans Fink and Alasdair MacIntyre (University of Notre Dame Press, 1977), p. 8.
3 Leon Shestov, 'All things are perishable', in *A Shestov Anthology*, ed. Bernard Martin (Ohio State University Press, 1970), p. 70.
4 Anthony Giddens, *The Transformation of Intimacy: Sexuality, Love and Eroticism in Modern Societies* (Polity, 1992), pp. 58, 137.
5 Knud Løgstrup, *After the Ethical Demand*, trans. Susan Dew and van Kooten Niekerk (Aarhus University, 2002), p. 26.
6 Ibid., p. 28.
7 Ibid., p. 25.
8 Ibid., p. 14.
9 Martin Heidegger, *Sein und Zeit*, first published in *Jahrbuch für Philosophie und Phänomenologische Forschung* (1926).
10 Løgstrup, *After the Ethical Demand*, pp. 4, 3.
11 Ibid., pp. 1–2.
12 G. Gumpert and S. Drucker, 'The mediated home in a global village', *Communication Research* 4 (1996), pp. 422–38.
13 Stephen Graham and Simon Marvin, *Splintering Urbanism* (Routledge, 2001), p. 285.
14 Ibid., p. 15.
15 M. Schwarzer, 'The ghost wards; the flight of capital from history', *Thresholds* 16 (1998), pp. 10–19.
16 M. Castells, *The Informational City* (Blackwell, 1989), p. 228.
17 Michael Peter Smith, *Transnational Urbanism: Locating Globalization* (Blackwell, 2001), pp. 54–5; and see John Friedman 'Where we stand: a decade of world city research', in P. L. Knox and P. J. Taylor (eds), *World Cities in a World System* (Cambridge University Press, 1995); David Harvey, 'From space to place and back again: reflections on the condition of postmodernity', in J. Bird et al. (eds), *Mapping the Futures* (Routledge, 1993).
18 Manuel Castells, *The Power of Identity* (Blackwell, 1997), pp. 61, 25.

19 Manuel Castells, 'Grassrooting the space of flows', in J. O. Wheeler, Y. Aoyama and B. Warf (eds), *Cities in the Telecommunications Age: The Fracturing of Geographies* (Routledge, 2000), pp. 20–1.

20 Smith, *Transnational Urbanism*, p. 108.

21 John Hannigan, *Fantasy City* (Routledge, 1998).

22 B. J. Widick, *Detroit: City of Race and Class Violence* (Wayne State University Press, 1989), p. 210.

23 Hannigan, *Fantasy City*, pp. 43, 51.

24 See Steve Proffitt's interview in *Los Angeles Times*, 12 Oct. 1997.

25 Michael Storper, *The Regional World: Territorial Development in a Global Economy* (Guilford Press, 1997), p. 235.

26 Teresa Caldeira, 'Fortified enclaves: the new urban segregation', *Public Culture* (1996), pp. 303–28.

27 Nan Elin, 'Shelter from the storm, or form follows fear and vice versa', in Nan Elin (ed.), *Architecture of Fear* (Princeton Architectural Press, 1997), pp. 13, 26.

28 Steven Flusty, 'Building paranoia', in Elin, *Architecture of Fear*, pp. 48–52.

29 Richard Sennett, *The Uses of Disorder: Personal Identity and City Life* (Faber, 1996), pp. 39, 42.

30 Ibid., p. 194.

31 See for instance William B. Beyer, 'Cyberspace or human space: whither cities in the age of telecommunications?', in Wheeler, Aoyama and Warf (eds), *Cities in the Telecommunications Age*, pp. 176–8.

4 Togetherness Dismantled

Another version of this chapter was published, under the title 'The fate of humanity in the post-Trinitarian world', in *Journal of Human Rights*, no. 3 (2002).

1 D. G. McNeil Jr, 'Politicians pander to fear of crime', *New York Times*, 5–6 May 2002.

2 See Nathaniel Herzberg and Cécile Prieur, 'Lionel Jospin et le "piège" sécuritaire', *Le Monde*, 5–6 May 2002.

3 Quoted by McNeil, 'Politicians pander to fear of crime'.

4 See *USA Today*, of 11 June 2002, particularly 'Al-Qaeda operative tipped off plot', 'US: dirty bomb plot foiled', and 'Dirty bomb plot: "The future is here, I'm afraid"'.

5 As Giorgio Agamben discovered, see his *Homo sacer. Il potere sovrano e la nuda vita* (Einaudi, 1995).

6 Giorgio Agamben, *Mezzi senza fine* (1996); here quoted after the translation by Vinzenzo Binetti and Cesare Casarino, *Means without Ends: Notes on Politics* (University of Minnesota Press, 2000), p. 20.

7 Edmund Burke, *Reflections on the Revolution in France* (1790), quoted by Arendt from the edition by E. J. Payne (Everyman's Library).

8 Hannah Arendt, *The Origins of Totalitarianism* (Andre Deutsch, 1986), pp. 300, 293.

9 See the translators' note in Agamben, *Means without Ends*, p. 143.

10 'Karl Jaspers: Citizen of the World?', in Hannah Arendt, *Men in Dark Times* (Harcourt Brace, 1993), pp. 81–94.

11 Agamben, *Means without Ends*, p. 21.

12 Victor W. Turner, *The Ritual Process: Structure and Anti-Structure* (Routledge, 1969), pp. 170, 96.

13 Hannah Arendt, 'On humanity in dark times: thoughts about Lessing', in *Men in Dark Times*, p. 15.

14 Carl Schmitt, *Theorie des Partisanen. Zwischenbemerkung zum Begriff des Politischen* (Duncker and Humboldt, 1963), p. 80. See the discussion in Giorgio Agamben, *Homo Sacer: Sovereign Power and Bare Life* (Stanford University Press, 1998), p. 137.

15 Carl Schmitt, *Politische Theologie. Vier Kapitel sur Lehre von der Souveränität* (Duncker and Humboldt, 1922), pp. 19–21. See the discussion in Agamben, *Homo Sacer*, pp. 15ff.

16 Agamben, *Homo Sacer*, p. 18.

17 Ibid., p. 142.

18 Arendt, *The Origins of Totalitarianism*, p. 204.

19 A charge eagerly resorted to, with great profit, by an ever widening range of contemporary politicians across the political spectrum, from Le Pen, Pia Kjersgaard or Vlaam Bloc on the far right to a growing number of those defining themselves as 'left of centre'.

20 See, for instance, the *Daily Mail* editorial of 5 August 2002 on the 'arrival here of scores of workers already suffering from the Aids virus'.

21 *Guardian*, 26 Nov. 2001.

22 See Michel Foucault, 'Of other spaces', *Diacritics* I (1986), p. 26.

23 See Alan Travis, 'UK plan for asylum crackdown', *Guardian*, 13 June 2002.

24 Gary Younge, 'Villagers and the damned', *Guardian*, 24 June 2002.

25 See Loïc Wacquant, 'Symbole fatale. Quand ghetto et prison se ressemblent et s'assemblent', *Actes de la Recherche en Sciences Sociales* (Sept. 2001), p. 43.

26 See Norbbert Elias and John L. Scotson, *The Established and the Outsiders: A Sociological Inquiry into Community Problems* (Frank Cass, 1965), particularly pp. 81 and 95.

27 Ibid.

28 See Loïc Wacquant, 'The new urban color line: the state and fate of the ghetto in postfordist America', in Craig J. Calhoun (ed.), *Social Theory and the Politics of Identity* (Blackwell, 1994); also 'Elias in the dark ghetto', *Amsterdams Sociologisch Tidjschrift* (Dec. 1997).

29 See Michel Agier, 'Entre guerre et ville', *Ethnography* 3 (2002), pp. 317–42.

30 The first stage consisting in the dismantling of the old identity, the third and last in assembling the new one: see Arnold van Gennep, *The Right of Passage* (Routledge and Kegan Paul, 1960); Turner, *The Ritual Process.*

31 Agamben, *Homo Sacer.*

32 Alain Finkielkraut, *L'Humanité perdu* (Seuil, 1996), p. 43.

33 David Held, 'Violence, law and justice in a global age', *Constellations* (Mar. 2002), pp. 74–88.

34 Arendt, 'On humanity in dark times' pp. 24–5, 15.

35 Ibid., pp. 26–7.

36 Arendt, *The Origins of Totalitarianism*, p. 272.

37 Arendt, 'On humanity in dark times', p. 31.

38 Franz Rosenzweig, *Understanding the Sick and the Healthy: A View of World, Man and God* (Harvard University Press, 1999), p. 14.

39 Quoted by Glatzer in ibid., p. 33, after William James, *Pragmatism* (London, 1907), p. 201. The intimate link between Rosenzweig and James's ideas was first suggested by Ernst Simon in 1953.

40 Jürgen Habermas observes, correctly, that the expectation of universal consensus is built into any conversation and that without such an expectation communication would be all but inconceivable; what he does not say, though, is that if consensus is believed to be reached in ideal circumstances because of a 'one and only truth' waiting to be discovered and agreed upon, then something else is 'built into' any act of communication: the tendency to render all but one of the conversationalists, together with the variety of views they hold and herald, redundant. Odo Marquard, in *Abschied vom Prinzipiellen* (Philipp Reclam, 1991), suggests that by this interpretation the ideal of 'undistorted communication' looks like a posthumous vengeance of solipsism . . .

41 See the chapter 'Living and dying in the planetary frontier-land', in my *Society under Siege* (Polity, 2002).